ASTRONOMY FOR KIDS

ASTRONOMY
FOR KIDS

HOW TO EXPLORE OUTER SPACE WITH BINOCULARS, A TELESCOPE, OR JUST YOUR EYES!

BRUCE BETTS, PhD

Foreword by Erica Colón, PhD

ROCKRIDGE
PRESS

Cover and Interior Designer: Merideth Harte
Art Manager: Amy Hartmann
Editor: Susan Randol
Production Editor: Andrew Yackira
Icon and Equipment Illustrations: Steve Mack
Author Photo: Jennifer Vaughn

ISBN: Print 978-1-64152-143-7 | eBook 978-1-64152-144-4

Printed in Canada

For the stars of my life, my sons Daniel and Kevin

CONTENTS

FOREWORD

As a science teacher who also creates engaging science curricula for students like you, I know that one of the most difficult aspects of teaching astronomy—besides not being able to take you on a field trip to space—is that students' and teachers' time together ends when the afternoon bell rings. This is a problem because we all know that the best time to see stars, planets, and constellations is in the evening when the Sun goes down. From the classroom, a teacher is able to share strategies for understanding the phases of the Moon, help you simulate the seasons with simple tools, and provide images and materials to help you build models of the solar system. However, if all that were enough to answer all your questions about space and how to become an astronomer, you wouldn't be holding this book right now.

Your curiosity tells me you're already a true scientist. A scientist tries to understand the world around them by asking questions and trying to find the answers. Your curiosity has led you to this book and to the path of becoming a great astronomer—a scientist who studies natural objects in space, such as the Sun, the Moon, planets, stars, and comets. However, when you look up into the night sky, you start to realize how GINORMOUS space is, and that's when your questions start to form. How in the world are you supposed to know the difference between a star and a planet? What is a shooting star? Why does it look like constellations move over time? What equipment do you need to study space? All of these are excellent questions, and I know you have more, which is why you are holding the perfect book to help you find the answers you're looking for. Why, you ask? Well, if it were me, and I had questions about space and the objects in it, I would definitely want to learn from a planetary scientist, just like Dr. Bruce Betts, who wrote *Astronomy for Kids* for you!

Many astronomers started out by looking up to the sky, and *Astronomy for Kids* is designed to be used as a take-along, sky-gazing reference tool. Whether you have a pair of binoculars, a telescope, or just your eyes, you can use the images on each page to help you find what you are looking for. Not only that, but once you find a constellation, or a cluster of stars, Dr. Betts will guide you on how to use that point to find another celestial body. And let's not forget the numerous cool facts he'll share throughout the book that will make you a hit on your next astronomy club outing. Wait, you don't have an astronomy club? Looks like I've just met the next astronomy club president in your area.

People have been exploring the night skies ever since someone first looked up, and astronomers are still making discoveries today. Now it's time for you to plan your own night watch, grab *Astronomy for Kids*, and head outside to start making your own discoveries among the stars.

—ERICA L. COLÓN, PhD
Founder of Nitty Gritty Science, LLC

INTRODUCTION

I have loved looking at the night sky since I was a small child. To this day, looking up and seeing familiar stars, constellations, and planets fills me with a sense of wonder and joy. They are like old friends that I can always rely on.

The night sky is beautiful, but it becomes fun and interesting as you learn how to find and identify certain stars and constellations, and how to watch the movement of the planets. You also can share what you learn with your friends and family, pointing out things in the sky and talking about what they are. You can say things like, "That's Jupiter," and "Those stars are the constellation Cygnus the Swan," and "That group of stars doesn't have a name but I think it looks like my dog getting belly rubs."

Many experts agree that the best way to start out in astronomy is to study the sky with just your eyes. You should get to know the sky and its objects before you move on to binoculars and telescopes. If you have them, binoculars and telescopes can then be used to bring out the details of these objects and to find other things that are not visible with just your eyes. For example, you can see the planet Saturn with just your eyes, its largest moon with binoculars, and its rings with a telescope.

This book starts with objects you can see with your eyes, then moves on to objects you can see with binoculars, then to objects you can see with a telescope. You'll learn about stars, constellations, planets, and other things and how to find them. You'll also get some general tips, learn about binoculars and telescopes, pick up some fun facts, and find out where you can learn more.

I started my journey in astronomy as a kid looking up at the night sky and learning what things were called. My curiosity kept growing. I learned more from books and from teachers and other adults. I got excited seeing the photos sent back by spacecraft that visited other worlds. I became interested in cool space facts, like one million Earths could fit inside the Sun, blue stars are hotter than red stars, and dogs live on Mars. Eventually, I studied astronomy and related sciences in school, where I learned dogs don't actually live on Mars (but I still think it would be cool if they did). I became a planetary scientist, which is exactly what it sounds like—someone who studies planets. I studied Mars and the moons of Jupiter, amazing worlds with giant volcanoes and canyons and surfaces made of ice. I used giant telescopes and spacecraft data, but I never lost the joy of just looking up at the sky and knowing that I was looking at Saturn, or Mars, or the brightest star in the night sky.

Now I enjoy sharing the wonder and excitement of the weird and cool things in outer space. I teach classes, give lectures, do a weekly radio show, make funny videos, and share information on social media. I have written this book to share the joy of astronomy with you. I hope you will use what you learn in this book to go outside, look up at the night sky, and have fun!

You can experience astronomy with just your own eyes. That is part of what makes it fun. You can actually go outside and *see* **STARS**, **PLANETS**, **CONSTELLATIONS**, and more in the night sky. You'll need to know what to look for, as well as when and where to look. I'll give you that information in later chapters, including using just your eyes (chapter 2), using binoculars (chapter 3), and using small telescopes (chapter 4). But first, in this chapter, I am going to start you on your way to becoming an astronomer with some general sky information and tips for observing. (Words that might be new to you, and that are defined in the glossary at the back of the book, will appear in bold type.)

TIPS FOR SEEING OUTER SPACE

There are a few things you can do to make it easier to see cool space stuff.

AVOID BAD SKIES

Let's start with something obvious: cloudy skies are bad for astronomy. Thick clouds make it impossible to see sky stuff, and thin clouds will block all but the brightest objects. You can't change the weather, but you can use weather predictions to choose nights that will likely be better for observing.

Bright skies are also bad. If you live in a city and have ever gone camping, you know you can see many more stars far from the city lights. Even if you live in a city, don't worry. A lot of the things I discuss in this book, such as bright stars and bright planets, will be visible from within most cities. But if you can get to a dark sky tens of miles (tens of kilometers) from a city, you'll be able to see more stars, and see more of the dimmer objects like **STAR CLUSTERS** and galaxies that we'll discuss in later chapters. But even just getting away from bright light concentrations like sports fields will help some.

The **MOON** can also make the sky bright and make it hard to see things. Sunlight reflects off the Earth's Moon. That is what we call moonlight. Particularly on nights near the Full Moon (when you see a lot of the Moon's face lit up), the moonlight makes the entire sky bright and we can't see as many stars. The best nights to look for dim things like a star cluster, a **NEBULA** (a cloud of gas and dust), or a **GALAXY** are when the Moon is not up or when it is only a crescent. If you are observing in the evening, plan to observe the night sky a few days after the Full Moon until a few days after the New Moon. Those are the days the Moon is not in the evening sky. You can find out when the Moon is full and when it is new on the Internet or find it in newspapers or astronomy magazines. But remember, you can see bright stars even when the Moon is bright.

GET THAT FLASHLIGHT OUT OF MY EYES

When you are in a bright room and the lights go off, you can't see very well at first. That's because your eyes were adjusted for bright light. After a few minutes, your eyes adjust and can see better in dim light. The same is true when you go out to look at the night sky. Your eyes will take some time to be able to see dim objects in the sky. You'll be able to see bright stars quickly, but your eyes will have to adjust to be able to see dim objects. Your eyes can take 30 minutes or more to be fully adjusted. And every time your eyes look at a bright light, whether it's a flashlight beam, a cell phone screen, or a porch light, your night vision will be ruined and your eyes will have to start adjusting all over again. So make sure you turn off all the lights you can, and keep them off, while you are looking at the sky.

However, there is a trick so you can still have light but not completely ruin your night vision. Red light does not affect your night vision as much as white light, so use a red flashlight, a flashlight covered with red cellophane, or the red night mode on astronomy apps. Even if you use red light, you should use dim red light if possible.

Since we're talking about eyes, I want to share another weird trick that can help you see dimmer objects. You won't need it for bright stars, but it can help you see the dimmer objects we'll get to later in the book like nebulae (the plural of nebula) and galaxies. Look just a little to the side of or above or below what you are trying to see, but concentrate on the location of what you are trying to see. Called averted vision, this trick can help because it avoids the least light-sensitive part of your eye. Using the more light-sensitive parts of your eye allows you to see dimmer objects.

LOOKING FOR COLOR

One of the interesting things to notice about objects in the night sky is their color. Even though your dark-adjusted vision won't see colors as well as your well-lit vision, you should be able to detect colors of brighter objects like stars and planets. Star colors depend on the temperature of the star. Although all stars are hot, really hot stars will be blue, and cooler stars will be red. Stars that are in between in temperature will be a different shade of blue or red, or just appear white. Planets vary in color depending on what they are made of. Mars is reddish orange and Saturn is yellow. So look for colors as you observe. In later chapters, when we talk about dimmer objects like nebulae, your eyes alone probably won't be able to detect much color because of the limits of our darkness-adapted vision.

Imagine a ball on the ground. Imagine a tiny person on top of the ball. That person will be able to see above and to the sides of the ball but not under the ball. The Earth is a sphere (shaped like a ball). So people in the Northern Hemisphere (the "top" of the ball in our example) see different parts of the sky than people in the Southern Hemisphere. One extreme case is if you are at the South Pole, you can't see the Northern sky at all. **THE OBJECTS IN THIS BOOK ARE VISIBLE FOR PEOPLE IN THE NORTHERN HEMISPHERE (NORTH OF EARTH'S EQUATOR), BUT NOT NECESSARILY FOR PEOPLE IN THE SOUTHERN HEMISPHERE.** This is particularly true of objects in the Northern part of the sky like the Big Dipper. **ALSO, REFERENCES TO SEASONS IN THIS BOOK ARE FOR NORTHERN HEMISPHERE SEASONS. SOME DETAILS GIVEN (FOR EXAMPLE, ABOUT HEIGHTS OF OBJECTS ABOVE THE HORIZON) ARE MOST ACCURATE FOR MID-NORTHERN LATITUDES, INCLUDING THE CONTINENTAL UNITED STATES.**

HEY, WHY DID THE SKY MOVE?

Where things are in the sky changes. These changes occur each night and from season to season. Let's find out why.

NIGHTLY CHANGES

You know how the Sun appears to move across the sky during the day? It rises in the Eastern sky and sets in the Western sky. The same thing happens with stars at night. During the night, most of the stars will move from East to West. The only exceptions are far in the Northern part of the sky, where stars will appear to rotate around what is known as the North Star. (You'll learn more about the North Star and how to find it on page 21.) All of these motions are actually caused by the Earth rotating like a spinning ball. But we are moving with the surface of the Earth, so to us it looks like the stars and the Sun are moving.

For the purposes of this book, there are two key points. One is just to know that the stars and other sky objects are moving. The other point is **WHEN I GIVE DIRECTIONS IN THE SKY, OR TELL YOU WHERE CONSTELLATIONS ARE DURING A CERTAIN SEASON, I ASSUME YOU ARE LOOKING DURING EVENING HOURS.** Positions of the objects will be different if you look later in the night or before dawn.

SUN CAUTION!

In the rest of this book, I talk only about the night sky, except when I discuss solar eclipses. But I want to make sure you know not to look directly at the Sun. Unlike everything in the night sky, looking directly at the Sun can damage your eyes, and even cause blindness. This is true even during the partial phases of solar eclipses. And don't ever point binoculars or a telescope at the Sun because that will damage your eyes and cause blindness almost immediately. There are special filters that can be used to observe the Sun, but they must be the right special filters. Do not even try observing the Sun without a knowledgeable adult who has the special proper equipment.

SEASONAL CHANGES

The Earth goes around the Sun once a year. Let's use our imaginations to understand what happens to the night sky over the course of a year.

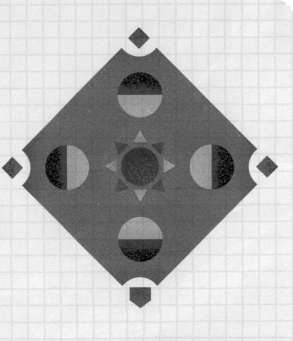

Imagine an indoor baseball stadium with a super bright light on the pitcher's mound (see diagram at right). That light represents the Sun. You will be the Earth and going around the bases will represent the Earth's **ORBIT** around the Sun. But you always have to face away from the bright light because your face is going to represent the night side of Earth, which is always the opposite side of the Earth from the Sun.

Each base represents the start of a season. Let's say home plate is Winter. Then, during the Winter, you can see the stands behind home plate and some of the first and third base dugouts. Then you head to first base (Spring). Now you see some of the stands in right field. Off to second base (Summer). Now you are looking at center field and can see the outfield stands. Notice that you can no longer see any of the stands behind home plate. And when you were at home plate, you couldn't see any of center field.

The night sky we can see works the same way. You can see stars and constellations in the Summer that you can't see at all in the Winter. Each season has stars, constellations, and other objects that are best viewed each year during that season.

BRIGHTNESS

Astronomers usually use a system that can seem really weird and confusing at first to measure how bright something is. You don't need to learn the system to use this book, but it can be very helpful when you look things up in other books, magazines, or on the Internet. Those sources will often tell you the brightness of a certain star or other object using what are called magnitudes. In order of importance, these are the things you should know about the magnitude system of brightness measurement (at least in my opinion):

1. Brighter objects have smaller numbers, so a star of magnitude 1 is brighter than a star of magnitude 2.

2. Sometimes brightness will be given by a number (magnitude 1) and sometimes by a so-called ordinal number (first magnitude). They mean the same thing.

3. Negative numbers are brighter than positive numbers. For example, the brightest night sky star is Sirius, which is about magnitude –1.5. Venus is even brighter, at about magnitude –4.

4. The dimmest star you can see with just your eyes from an extremely dark site is about magnitude 6. If you are in a city, you may only be able to see objects that are magnitude 2 or brighter, or if the light pollution is really bad, only objects that are magnitude 1 or brighter.

5. Each difference of one magnitude represents a big jump in brightness—a factor of 2.512, to be exact. This means that if one star is five magnitudes brighter than another, it is 100 times brighter. So a magnitude 1 star is 100 times brighter than a magnitude 6 star.

Let's go back to imagining the baseball field. First, imagine your head is always tilted up some, and you can choose to tilt it up a lot. In a very approximate way, that simulates being in the middle part of the Northern Hemisphere—for example, in the United States or most of Europe. Now, in the imaginary baseball field, notice that if you look all the way up, no matter what base you are on, you can see some of the same parts of the stadium roof. That represents the part of the sky you can see year-round—the Northern parts of our sky as seen in the Northern Hemisphere.

In each chapter of this book, the objects are organized either by the best season to observe them, or as Northern Sky objects, meaning they are visible all year. Each object will have banners representing the best season to observe it or noting that it is a Northern Sky object.

What's that? Yes, you can finish going around the bases. You reach third base (Autumn), then cross home plate (Winter) after a simulated year.

HOW DO I FIND STUFF?

I'll give you various ways to find things in the night sky. In this book, each object, like a star or a collection of stars, will have a simulated picture to show what it looks like or where it is relative to other stars. That can be enough to find it. Or I may use one group of stars—the Big Dipper, for example—to point you to something else, like the North Star. The following information also can help you find stuff in the sky.

DETERMINING DIRECTION IN THE SKY

You should learn how to determine what direction you are looking: North, East, South, West, or somewhere in between. That can be helpful in finding something in the sky. It is also a good thing to know in life. Often, the easiest direction to find first is North. You can use a compass—either an actual compass or a properly adjusted phone compass—that tells you where North is. Or you can use a map if you know where you are and which way you are facing relative to the map. Or, my personal favorite, you can use the sky itself! On pages 19 and 21, I'll teach you how to find the star pattern called the Big Dipper and from that how to find Polaris, also known as the North Star. The North Star is always North. Once you are facing North, West is on your left, East is on your right, and South is behind you.

MEASURING ANGLES IN THE SKY

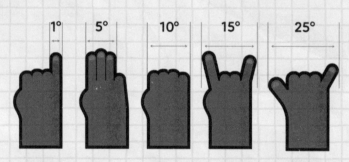

It's very useful to learn how to approximate angles between things in the sky— basically how far apart two objects are in the sky. I will sometimes mention how far apart things are using angles measured in degrees. There are 360 degrees in a circle—in other words, if you spin around all the way and stop exactly where you started. The great thing is you can use your hands to approximate angles. Hold your arm out straight, with your fist closed, and point it where you want to measure in the sky. From one edge of your closed fist to the other edge is about 10 degrees. If you spread your fingers out, the tip of your thumb to the tip of your little finger is about 22 to 25 degrees. The tip of your little finger is about 1 degree, and your three middle fingers together are about 5 degrees. These are not exact measurements, but they can help get you to the right part of the sky. Remember to keep your arm straight when measuring.

KEEP IN MIND

Along with ways to see outer space and how to find the objects you're looking for, you need to know a few additional pieces of information.

WORD PLAY: CONSTELLATIONS, ASTERISMS, AND CLUSTERS

An **ASTERISM** is any group of stars that anyone thinks makes a pattern in the sky—for example, the Big Dipper. When I use the term *constellation*, I am referring to one of the 88 modern constellations. Constellations are also collections of stars that make a pattern in the sky, but they are the formally agreed-upon patterns with agreed-upon names. They are usually bigger than what are referred to as asterisms. Constellations also have boundaries, kind of like countries do. When put together, the area of the 88 constellations make up the entire *celestial sphere*, which is the sky as seen from both the Northern and Southern Hemispheres and covering all seasons. When I talk about a star in this book, I will usually tell you what constellation the star is in. You can think of this like cities and states. When you are talking about a city, including the state tells you what part of the country it is in. It is the same thing with constellations. Specifying a constellation when you talk about a star tells you what part of the sky the star is in.

We'll also talk about and see star clusters. A star cluster is a group of stars that not only appear near one another in the sky but are also near one another in space. There are two types: **OPEN CLUSTERS** and **GLOBULAR CLUSTERS**.

A NOTE ABOUT PLANETS

Several planets are bright and easy to see, but you have to know where to look because they move around the sky throughout the year and from year to year. The word *planet* comes from the Greek word meaning "wanderer." Planets appear to wander around more than the stars, which don't move relative to one another. (Well, technically they do, but that is only easily noticeable over hundreds or thousands of years, so I wouldn't worry about it.) In this book I'll describe what the planets look like and what times of night they can appear. To know where to look on a certain day, you'll have to use the Resources section of this book where I list websites, magazines, computer software, apps, and other things that can tell you where to find the planets.

A MESS OF MESSIER OBJECTS

For many of the objects discussed later in this book, you'll see that after their name they'll have an "M" followed by a number—for example, the Andromeda Galaxy (M31). In the 1700s, an astronomer named Charles Messier numbered the fuzzy-looking objects he could see in the sky with or without his telescope. The numbers stuck and now they are called Messier numbers. Sometimes astronomers just refer to the objects by Messier number rather than name, so I included them in this book.

TOOLS AND SUPPLIES

What do you take with you when you go out sky watching? I offer some suggestions next, but these items are optional. The only things you truly need are you and your curiosity. But taking some of these might help your astronomy and your comfort. The Resources section at the end of the book has more information about astronomy items.

ASTRONOMY STUFF

> This book ☺
> A red flashlight or flashlight covered in red cellophane so you don't ruin your night vision
> Seasonal sky charts—for example, if it's Winter, you could take a chart of the Winter sky
> Any night sky apps you have that point out or help you find constellations—be sure to run them in night mode to help your night vision
> A laptop computer in night mode running a night sky program
> A planisphere, which is a handheld sky chart you can adjust to match the season and time
> Binoculars
> Telescope and instructions

COMFORT STUFF

> Warm clothing if it is cold or might get cold
> Snacks
> Bug repellent, if there are biting bugs out
> A chair, ideally a reclining one
> A blanket or mattress to spread on the ground
> A pillow

The information from this chapter will help you become a better astronomer, and that will make observing the night sky more fun. Now we can move on to what to see.

> CHAPTER 2

USE YOUR EYES

You don't need equipment to see some of the most spectacular sights in the universe. You can just use your eyes. Use the knowledge and tips you learned in chapter 1 along with the information you'll find in this chapter to get to know the joy and wonder of the night sky.

THE BIG 30

These are my top 30 things to see with just your eyes. They are all interesting and most are bright and easy to observe. The objects are organized into groups based on either the best season to view them or by the kind of object it is (for things like planets, whose positions don't change consistently with season). Each object gets its own page that discusses it and how to find it. The pages are organized in the following order:

> The Northern Sky (objects visible year-round or nearly year-round)
> The Winter Sky
> The Spring Sky
> The Summer Sky
> The Autumn Sky
> Planets
> Oddballs: The Moon and the Milky Way
> Occasional Sights

I suggest you start with the objects listed in the Northern Sky section (page 18), and the objects listed in whatever season it is for you right now. You can also observe whatever planets are currently visible (see the Resources section at the back of the book to find where you can learn what planets are visible). If you are at a dark site, read about the Milky Way, and if the Moon is up, check out that page. And look at the Occasional Sights section (page 72) to learn about other things you can sometimes see, including eclipses, **METEOR** showers, and the International Space Station.

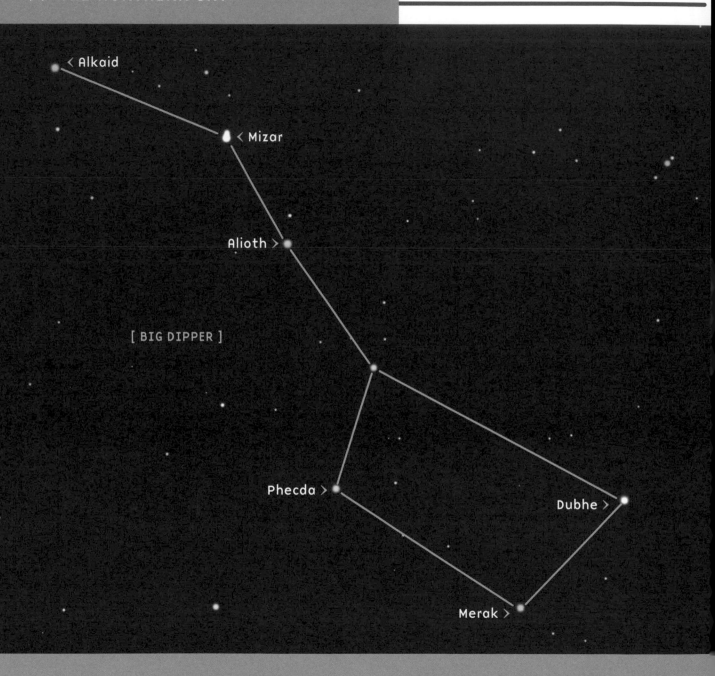

THE BIG DIPPER

Probably the most recognizable pattern of stars in the Northern Hemisphere is the Big Dipper, a collection of seven relatively bright stars. It got its name from people who thought it looked like a "dipper," or a ladle or big spoon. It is one part of the constellation Ursa Major (which means "Greater Bear").

The Big Dipper is always approximately in the North, though depending on the time of year and time of night, it may be in the Northeast or Northwest or low down near the horizon. From most of the Northern Hemisphere, it is visible year-round. If you have trouble finding it, you can use a star chart to help (see the Resources section).

As you'll discover in the following pages, once you locate the Big Dipper, you can use it to find other things, including Polaris (the North Star).

> THAT'S SO COOL!

The Big Dipper is referred to in different ways around the world. In the United Kingdom, it is often called the Plough. In the Netherlands, it is sometimes called the Great Bear (tied to Ursa Major), but it is more commonly known there as the Saucepan.

Merak >

[BIG DIPPER]

Dubhe >

Alkaid ^

< Polaris

POLARIS
(THE NORTH STAR)

If you can find the star Polaris, you will know where North is. Polaris, called the North Star, is always North. The other stars will appear to rotate around Polaris during the night.

As shown in the illustration to the left, to find Polaris draw a line through the two stars making up the outside of the cup of the Big Dipper, named Merak and Dubhe, and keep going until the line runs into a somewhat bright star—that is Polaris.

Polaris is always North, so now as long as it isn't cloudy, you can always find North at night.

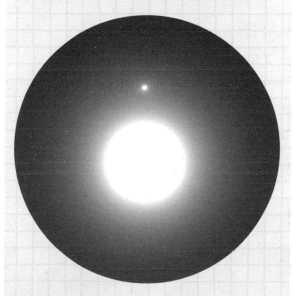

> An artist's idea of what the bright and large Polaris and its very close dwarf (small) star companion look like.

USE YOUR EYES

[CASSIOPEIA]

Caph >

CASSIOPEIA

Cassiopeia, "the Queen," is an easy-to-find constellation that looks like a "W" or an "M," depending on the season and the time of night. To find it, use the stars of the Big Dipper (page 19) to draw a line to the North Star (as discussed on page 21), then keep going with the line and you will reach one end of Cassiopeia, a star named Caph.

Like all other constellations, Cassiopeia rotates around the North Star during the night because of the Earth's rotation. In the evening hours, during the Winter, Cassiopeia looks like an "M" above the North Star, and during the Summer it looks like a "W" below the North Star.

(page 19) ... page 21)

> THAT'S SO COOL!

In Greek mythology, Cassiopeia was a queen who was made into a constellation by the sea god Poseidon for claiming she was more beautiful than the sea nymphs.

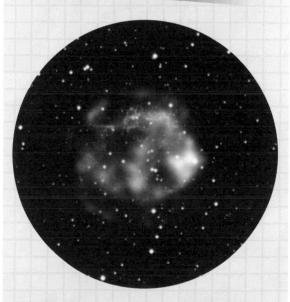

> *Within Cassiopeia is Cassiopeia A, a supernova remant—expanding clouds of stuff from the explosion of a large star. This image was produced using the NuSTAR space telescope that detects X-rays, which are not visible with your eyes.*

Pollux >

< Capella

Procyon >

< Betelgeuse

< Aldebaran

Sirius >

< Rigel

THE WINTER HEXAGON

The Winter Hexagon (a six-sided shape) is an asterism formed by six bright stars that cover a large portion of the Southern sky in the Winter.

Starting with the brightest star in the sky (page 29) and going clockwise, the six stars and their constellations are Sirius in Canis Major (page 29), Procyon in Canis Minor, Pollux in Gemini (page 35), Capella in Auriga, Aldebaran in Taurus (page 31), and Rigel in Orion (page 27). The bright star Betelgeuse, also part of the constellation Orion, is inside the hexagon. You can use the shape of the hexagon to find the stars and constellations, or use the individual stars and constellations to find the hexagon.

(page 29), (page 29), (page 35), (page 31), and Rigel in Orion (page 27)

> ## THAT'S SO COOL!

The Winter Hexagon is sometimes called the Winter Football because of its shape and because it is easily visible at the end of the National Football League season in late January and early February.

> A picture of the Winter Hexagon.

USE YOUR EYES

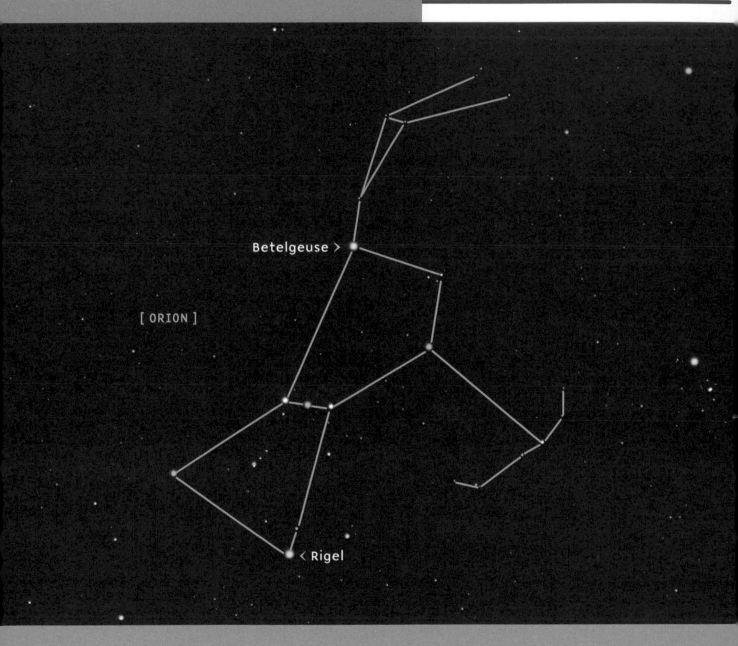

Betelgeuse >

[ORION]

< Rigel

> You won't see this (opposite page) with just your eyes, but the WISE telescope produced the infrared light image of multiple glowing gas and dust nebulae. The largest is the Flame Nebula. The star in the right part of the bright area in the picture is the left star in Orion's Belt, called Alnitak.

ORION,
INCLUDING THE STARS BETELGEUSE AND RIGEL

The constellation Orion, "the Hunter," is one of the coolest-looking constellations and one of the easiest to find in the Winter and early Spring. In the early evening, it will be in the Southeast in the beginning of Winter and in the Southwest by Spring.

Orion is easily identified by the three bright stars in a line that make up Orion's Belt. Combined with the belt, four other bright stars form sort of an hourglass shape that represents the main parts of Orion's body. Also particularly notable are its two brightest stars, Betelgeuse (upper left, his shoulder) and Rigel (lower right, his foot). When you look at them, notice that Betelgeuse is reddish in color. It is a **RED GIANT** star. Notice that Rigel is blue, indicating it is extremely hot, even for

a star. Redder stars like Betelgeuse are still hot, but they are cooler than blue stars.

> THAT'S SO COOL!

In *Harry Potter and the Order of the Phoenix*, the students say they see Orion in June near midnight during their Astronomy exam, but it is not possible to see Orion then.

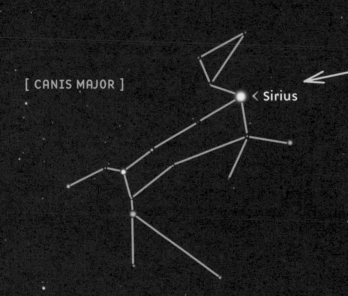

[CANIS MAJOR]

< Sirius

SIRIUS
WITHIN CANIS MAJOR

Sirius is the brightest star in the sky besides the Sun. It is in the constellation Canis Major, which means "Greater Dog." Because of that, Sirius is often called the Dog Star.

To find Sirius, just draw a line through the three stars of Orion's Belt to the left and in about 20 degrees look for the brightest star in the night sky.

> THAT'S SO COOL!

According to Greek mythology, the dog constellations Canis Major and Canis Minor, which means "Lesser Dog," are Orion's hunting dogs, following him through the sky. Must be ruff.

[TAURUS]

Aldebaran >

TAURUS,
INCLUDING THE STAR ALDEBARAN

The constellation Taurus, "the Bull," can be found by starting with Orion (page 27). Draw a line through the three stars of Orion's Belt and head right about 20 degrees. A little above that line will be a bright reddish star. That is Aldebaran, the Bull's eye. Aldebaran and some dimmer stars form a triangle marking the head of Taurus. Other faint stars extending out from the triangle form a "V" shape that is supposed to be Taurus's two horns.

We'll use Taurus to find the Pleiades and Hyades star clusters (pages 33 and 89).

(pages 33 and 89).

> ## THAT'S SO COOL!
> In some versions of mythology, Taurus the Bull is battling Orion the Hunter.

> *The bright red star Aldebaran with some of the Hyades star cluster.*

USE YOUR EYES

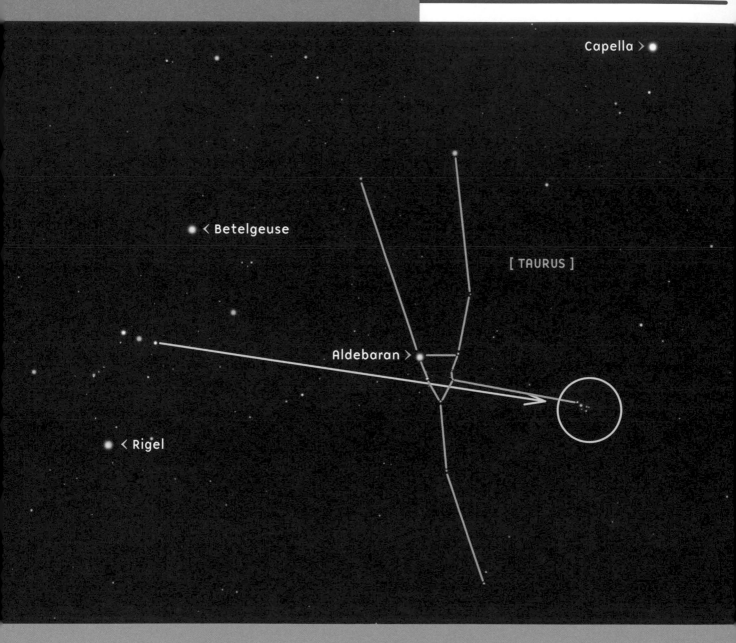

Capella >

< Betelgeuse

[TAURUS]

Aldebaran >

< Rigel

> The Pleiades (opposite page) as seen by the WISE space telescope using infrared light. The part of the infrared light that is sensitive to the heated dust clouds surrounding the stars has been coded green and red.

THE PLEIADES STAR CLUSTER (M45)

The Pleiades, "the Seven Sisters," is the easiest star cluster to identify in the sky with just your eyes. It is a group of relatively young stars that formed in the same region of space at about the same time.

To find them, draw a line through Orion's Belt (page 27) to the right and go about 10 degrees past the reddish star Aldebaran. The Pleiades will look like a small group of stars that are not very bright but are all similar in brightness. Depending on sky conditions, it may look like only a fuzzy or cloudy patch. Or you may be able to see five, six, or seven stars that look kind of like a tiny dipper. The seven stars led to the cluster being called the Seven Sisters based on the seven sisters of Greek mythology.

With binoculars, you can see tens of stars in the Pleiades and with a good telescope, you might be able to see hundreds.

> ## THAT'S SO COOL!

The Japanese word for Pleiades is *Subaru*, which is how the car company got its name. The symbol on a Subaru car is based on the Pleiades Cluster.

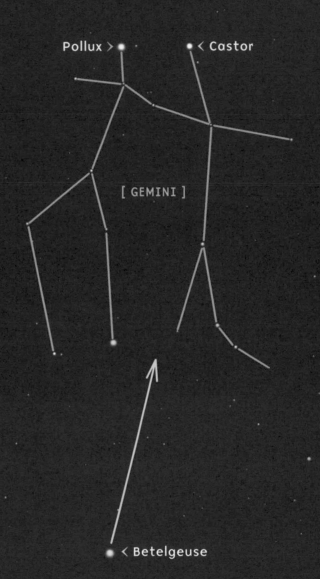

Pollux > ● ● < Castor

[GEMINI]

● < Procyon

● < Betelgeuse

GEMINI,
INCLUDING THE STARS CASTOR AND POLLUX

The constellation Gemini, "the Twins," is dominated by the two bright stars, Castor and Pollux, who are twins in Greek mythology.

To find Gemini, start with Orion (page 27) and draw a line between its two brightest stars, from Rigel to Betelgeuse, and continue that line about 30 degrees (three fist widths at arm's length). You will then be in the area of blue-white Castor and the brighter yellow-orange Pollux. Pollux can also be found from its position in the Winter Hexagon (page 25). Fainter stars heading toward Orion make up the bodies of the twins.

(page 27)
(page 25)

> THAT'S SO COOL!

Gemini is one of the constellations of the zodiac: an area of the sky through which the Sun appears to move over the course of a year. If you note where the Sun is relative to the constellations every day at midday, the Sun appears to move from day to day along a path through the zodiac, spending some of those days in Gemini. The actual motion is due to the Earth revolving around the Sun. From Earth, planets also appear in the sky at locations within the zodiac, so sometimes they will appear in Gemini, too.

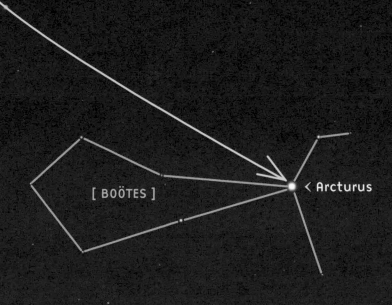

[BOÖTES]

< Arcturus

ARCTURUS
THE STAR WITHIN BOÖTES

Arcturus is the fourth brightest star in the night sky, behind only Sirius in brightness in the visible sky of the Northern Hemisphere.

It's easy to find by starting at the Big Dipper (page 19). Draw a curving line, also known as an arc, through the handle stars in the dipper. Continue following that curve for about 30 degrees and you'll come to the very bright and orange-colored Arcturus. A common way to remember this is "arc to Arcturus."

Arcturus and much dimmer stars that are kind of kite-shaped make up the constellation Boötes, "the Herdsman."

> ## > THAT'S SO COOL!
> Arcturus is a red giant star. A red giant is one of the end phases of some stars in which the star gets much bigger, and as a result, its surface cools, causing the red color. Arcturus has a diameter 25 times bigger than the Sun.

> The bright star Arcturus as seen through a telescope. The lines coming from the star are not real but are effects of the internal parts of the telescope.

< Arcturus

[VIRGO]

< Spica

SPICA
THE STAR WITHIN VIRGO

Spica is a bright blue-white star in the constellation Virgo, "the Maiden."

Spica is easy to find once you have found Arcturus (page 37). Start by following the curve of the handle stars of the Big Dipper and go 30 degrees to Arcturus. Then straighten the curve out a bit and go another 30 degrees and you will reach Spica. Remember this path as "arc to Arcturus," and then "speed on (or spike) to Spica."

The other stars in Virgo are rather dim, or to use a technical term, rather *lame*. But Spica shines brightly.

> ## > THAT'S SO COOL!
> Virgo is the second-largest constellation, after Hydra.

[LEO]

< Regulus

REGULUS
THE STAR WITHIN LEO

Regulus is a bright blue-white star in the constellation Leo, "the Lion," which includes several relatively bright stars. Leo's outline actually resembles a lion, unlike many constellations where it is hard to visualize what they are supposed to look like.

To find Regulus and Leo, use the outside cup stars (Dubhe and Merak) of the Big Dipper (page 19). Draw a line "down" through those cup stars—in other words, the opposite direction from the North Star (page 21)—and follow that line about 40 degrees to Leo's head. Or just look East in the evening at the beginning of Spring, moving to high in the South by mid to late Spring.

Leo's head looks like a backward question mark and the dot at the bottom of the question mark is Regulus. The rear portion of Leo is made up of a triangle of stars. I can imagine Leo as a lion lying down. What about you?

> ## THAT'S SO COOL!
In Greek mythology, Leo was identified as the Nemean Lion, which was killed by Heracles (Hercules to the Romans) during the first of his 12 labors.

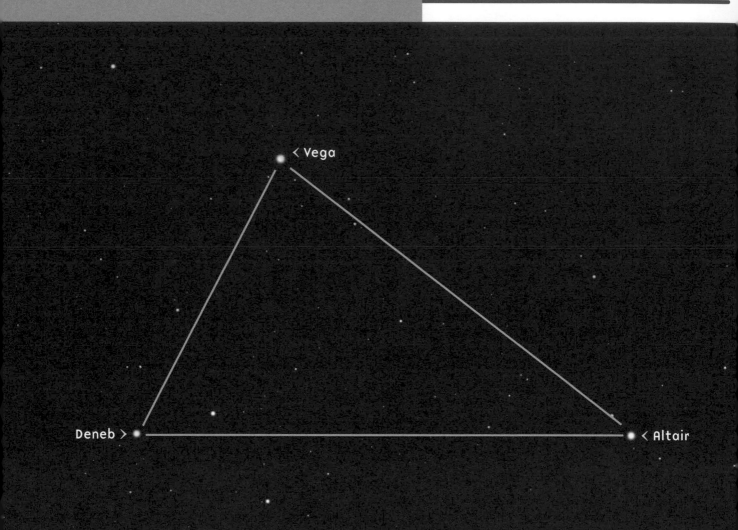

THE SUMMER TRIANGLE

The Summer Triangle is formed by three bright stars that become easily visible at the start of Summer. The triangle is large—about 30 degrees long and 20 degrees high. The three bright stars are Vega in the constellation Lyra, "the Lyre," Deneb in Cygnus, "the Swan," and Altair in Aquila, "the Eagle."

In early Summer the triangle is low on the Eastern horizon in the evening, but by mid to late Summer it is high overhead. It stays visible in the West into Autumn.

> THAT'S SO COOL!

Vega, the fifth brightest star in the night sky, is the brightest of the three stars in the Summer Triangle and is almost exactly zero magnitude (a measure of how bright it is).

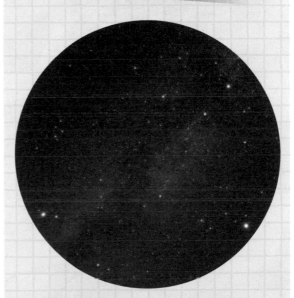

> An image of the Summer Triangle. In this picture, Vega is at the lower right. Note the Milky Way (page 71) can be seen within the triangle as well.

CYGNUS

The constellation Cygnus, "the Swan," includes the star Deneb of the Summer Triangle (page 43). Imagine Cygnus as a flying swan with a long neck. Deneb is the tail of the swan.

The constellation is cross-shaped. In fact, if you don't include the dimmer stars on the outer parts of the swan's wings, the remaining stars form the asterism known as the Northern Cross.

(page 43)

> ## > THAT'S SO COOL!
> There is a Southern Cross (the constellation Crux) visible from the Southern Hemisphere.

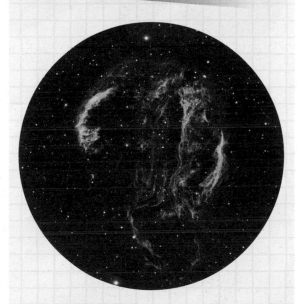

> Within Cygnus is the Cygnus Loop Nebula, shown above as seen in ultraviolet light by the GALEX space telescope. The hot gas and dust glow bright in ultraviolet light.

Antares >

[SCORPIUS]

> An image of the nebula DG 129 (opposite page) as seen by the WISE space telescope in infrared light. DG 129 is not very apparent at visible wavelengths (what your eye sees), but it stands out in infrared light.The bright star at the right is the right "claw" star of Scorpius.

SCORPIUS,
INCLUDING THE STAR ANTARES

Scorpius is a very recognizable Summer constellation that (with some imagination) looks like a scorpion, which is where its name comes from. Its body and tail are formed by a set of stars that make a "J" or fishhook shape. Near the top of its body is the bright reddish star Antares, a red giant star sometimes called the heart of the scorpion. Three fairly bright stars that are almost in a line form its head and claws.

The easiest way to find Scorpius is to look South on a July or August evening. Scorpius is always very low in the sky, getting about only 20 degrees above the horizon. But Scorpius's distinctive shape and the bright red Antares make it hard to miss as long as you have a clear view to the South during mid-Summer.

> ## > THAT'S SO COOL!
> The Sun is huge. Antares is super enormously gigantically impossible-to-imagine huge. If it were where the Sun is in our Solar System, the outer parts of Antares would extend out beyond the orbit of Mars.

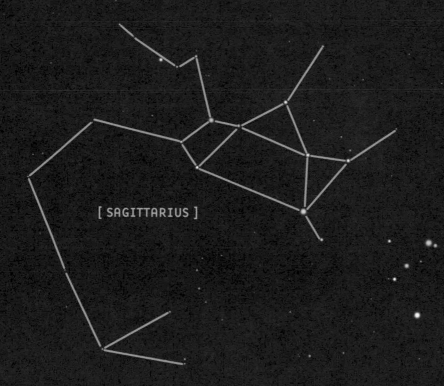

[SAGITTARIUS]

Antares >

SAGITTARIUS,
INCLUDING THE TEAPOT ASTERISM

Sagittarius is supposed to be a centaur archer—a half-man, half-horse creature with a bow. I find it hard to picture this in the stars of the Sagittarius constellation. But, what is much easier to find is an asterism within Sagittarius that looks like a teapot, complete with a handle, lid, and spout.

The easiest way to find Sagittarius is to look in late Summer, just to the left of Scorpius (page 47), low above the Southern horizon. Look for the teapot getting ready to pour tea on the scorpion's tail. Or maybe it's a centaur archer getting ready to shoot the heart of the scorpion. Or maybe it's something else. What do you think?

> ## THAT'S SO COOL!
If you could go really, really far (about 26,000 light years) in the direction of Sagittarius, you'd reach the center of our own Milky Way Galaxy.

> An image of the center of the Lagoon Nebula (page 147) within Sagittarius as seen by the Hubble Space Telescope. The picture shows dark dust and hazy gas clouds.

USE YOUR EYES

Alpheratz >

Enif >

[PEGASUS]

PEGASUS, INCLUDING THE GREAT SQUARE OF PEGASUS

A Pegasus is a mythological flying horse. In the constellation of Pegasus, the easiest thing to identify is an asterism of four relatively bright stars that form a square. It must be a really great square because it often is called the Great Square of Pegasus.

The square represents the Pegasus's body, which seems weird for a horse, but great for something to identify in the sky. You may also be able to distinguish the head and front legs of Pegasus, or at least you might if you realize the Pegasus is flying upside down. I suppose if we are going to believe in a flying horse, we might as well believe it is flying upside down. In October and November, Pegasus flies upside down high in the South.

Another way to find Pegasus is to draw a line from the two stars making up the outside of the cup of the Big Dipper (page 19) to Polaris (page 21), then on to Caph, a star in Cassiopeia. Then go about the same distance again (about 30 degrees) and you will come approximately to the star Alpheratz, which is one corner of the Great Square of Pegasus.

USE YOUR EYES

< Algol

[ANDROMEDA]

Mirach >

Alpheratz >

Hamal >

> The Andromeda Galaxy (opposite page) as seen in ultraviolet light by the GALEX space telescope. What it looks like in visible light (what you can see with your eyes) is discussed on page 95.

ANDROMEDA

In mythology, Andromeda was the daughter of Cassiopeia (page 23). In the sky, Andromeda is not a very obvious constellation, but it does contain the very interesting Andromeda Galaxy, which we will talk about in chapter 3 (page 81).

The easiest way to find Andromeda is to first find the Great Square of Pegasus (page 51). Andromeda shares the star Alpheratz with Pegasus. It's kind of funny that Alpheratz is the top of Andromeda's head and the rear end of the Pegasus.

To make the constellation Andromeda even more confusing, different sources draw the lines differently between the stars. One version is shown in the illustration to the left.

> ## THAT'S SO COOL!

In Greek mythology, Andromeda is linked to several other constellations. She was the daughter of Cassiopeia and Cepheus and was rescued from the sea monster Cetus by Perseus. Cassiopeia, Cetus, and Perseus are all names of constellations.

Fomalhaut >

[PISCIS AUSTRINUS]

FOMALHAUT
THE STAR IN PISCIS AUSTRINUS

The bright star Fomalhaut, "the Fish's Mouth," stands out because it is by far the brightest star in the Southern sky in Autumn. No similarly bright stars are anywhere near it. In fact, the other stars in its constellation are not bright at all.

Fomalhaut is part of the constellation Piscis Austrinus, which means "Southern Fish" (not to be confused with the constellation Pisces), and it derives from the Arabic words meaning "the fish's mouth." To find Fomalhaut, look for the only bright star in the Southeast in October and the South in November.

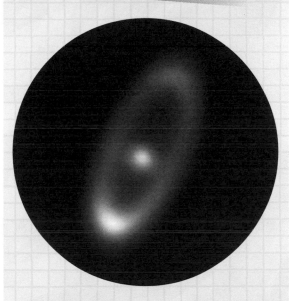

> *The star Fomalhaut as seen in infrared light by the Herschel space telescope. Surrounding the star is a dusty debris disk possibly formed by the collisions of comets with one another.*

USE YOUR EYES

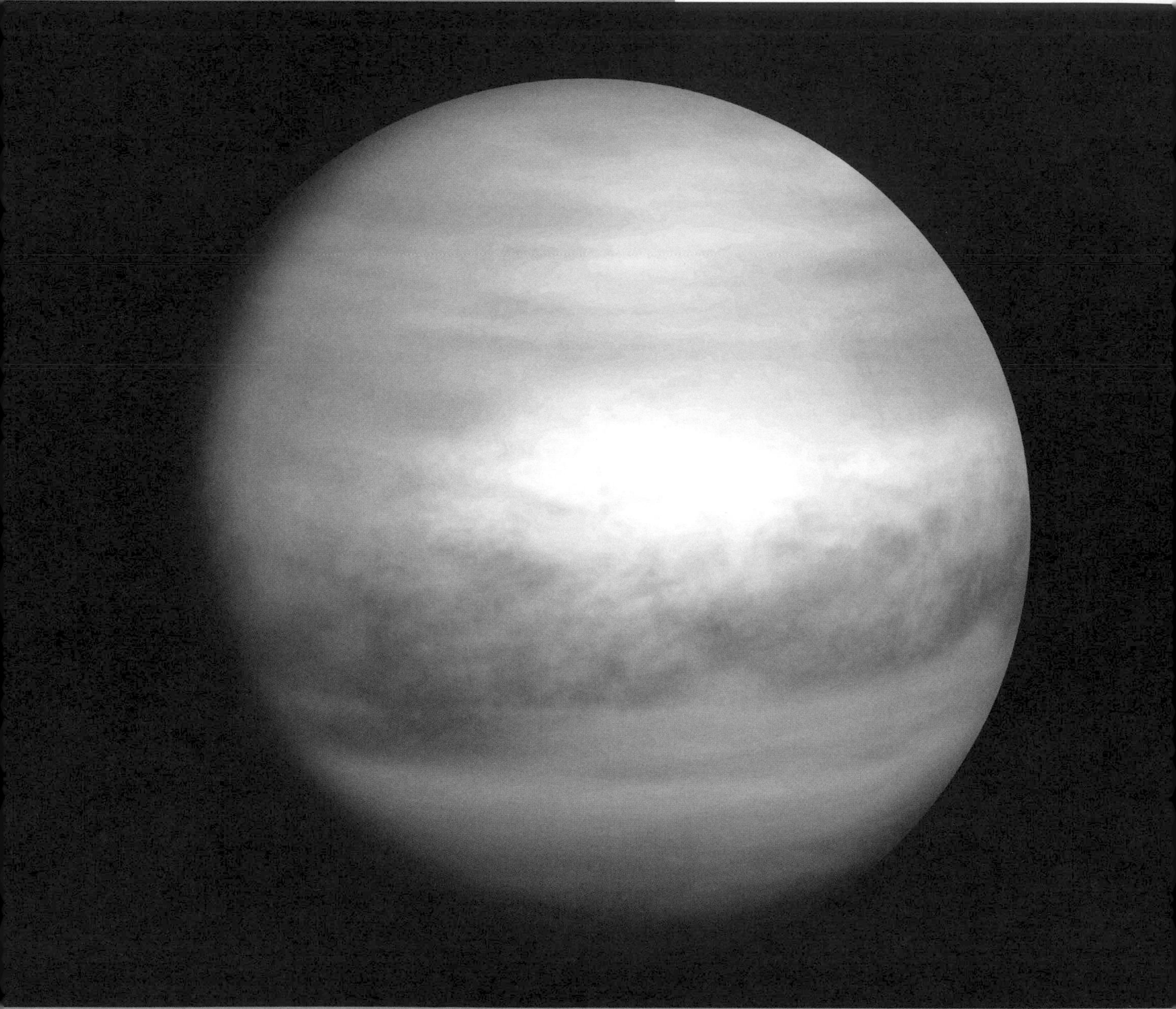

VENUS

The planet Venus is the brightest natural object in the night sky besides the Moon. In the sky, Venus looks like an extremely bright star. Venus is many times brighter than the brightest star, Sirius. Venus is similar in size to Earth, but has a much thicker **ATMOSPHERE** and a very hot surface. It is surrounded by bright clouds that reflect a lot of the sunlight that hits it—which is part of the reason it's so bright.

Venus is closer to the Sun than Earth (only Mercury is closer). Because of that we will see Venus usually in either the early evening or in the hours before dawn. During the middle of the night, we are looking away from the direction of the Sun and thus also away from the approximate direction of Venus.

You may sometimes see Venus in the evening sky, appearing low in the West after sunset, and sometimes in the morning sky, appearing low in the East before sunrise.

To know when and where to look for Venus, you'll need to check out the Internet, magazines, astronomy software, or apps. See the Resources section for more information.

> ## THAT'S SO COOL!
At almost 900 degrees Fahrenheit (almost 500 degrees Celsius), the surface temperature on Venus is much hotter than the hottest kitchen oven.

> *Jupiter as viewed by the Hubble Space Telescope in 2017. Notice the numerous cloud features.*

JUPITER

Only the Moon and Venus are brighter than Jupiter in the night sky. The fifth planet from the Sun, Jupiter is much farther away than Venus, but much larger so it still looks bright. (We see sunlight reflected off its clouds.) Jupiter is by far the largest planet in our Solar System. It will look to your eyes like an extremely bright star.

Jupiter is one of the gas giants: it is made almost entirely of gas. It is about five times farther from the Sun than Earth is.

With binoculars, you can see Jupiter's four largest moons (page 101). With a telescope, you may be able to see some of its colored cloud stripes (page 133).

To know when and where to look for Jupiter, you'll need to check the Internet, magazines, or astronomy software or apps. See the Resources section for more information.

> THAT'S SO COOL!

Jupiter is so big that all the other planets in our Solar System would easily fit inside it at the same time, and they'd have lots of room left over.

> A Juno spacecraft image of Jupiter's Great Red Spot, a hurricane-like storm that is bigger than Earth and has lasted for hundreds of years.

USE YOUR EYES

59

> An image of Mars as seen by the Viking orbiters. Many cloud-free pictures were combined to create this. Note the North Polar ice cap at the very top, the giant canyon system Valles Marineris toward the bottom, and the volcano Olympus Mons, which can be seen near the left edge of the planet.

MARS

The distance from Earth to Mars changes quite a lot as Earth and Mars orbit the Sun. Because of that, the brightness of Mars varies. Sometimes it looks like a sort of bright star. But when Mars and Earth are closest, which occurs every 26 months, Mars will look like an extremely bright star—brighter than the brightest night sky star, Sirius.

No matter how bright it is, Mars will appear orange or red to your eye. Mars, the fourth planet from the Sun, is known as the Red Planet because of its red color, which is caused by the rusty, red rocks and dust on its surface.

Through a medium-sized telescope, you might be able to see dark marks on Mars's surface or its white polar caps.

To know when and where to look for Mars, you'll need to check the Internet, magazines, or astronomy software or apps. See the Resources section for more information.

> THAT'S SO COOL!

Mars has the largest mountain in the Solar System, the volcano Olympus Mons. It is more than twice as high as Mount Everest and is as large as the state of Arizona.

> A selfie the Curiosity rover took on the surface of Mars in 2016 when it was next to a sand dune.

USE YOUR EYES

> The image above is a mosaic (a combination of pictures) from the Cassini mission to Saturn. It shows the planet and its rings, and some of Saturn's moons, which appear as white dots around it.

SATURN

Saturn, the sixth planet from the Sun, appears in the sky as a fairly bright, yellowish star, but will appear much dimmer than Venus or Jupiter.

Like any planet farther out from the Sun than the Earth, Saturn can be visible at any time of night, or not visible, depending on where Earth and Saturn are in their orbits around the Sun.

Saturn, like Jupiter, is a gas giant, so it is big and made mostly of gas with no solid ground.

With binoculars, you may be able to see Saturn's largest moon, Titan (page 103). With a telescope, you may be able to see Saturn's famous rings (page 131).

To know when and where to look for Saturn, you'll need to check the Internet, magazines, or astronomy software or apps. See the Resources section for more information.

(page 103)
(page 131)

> THAT'S SO COOL!

Though smaller than Jupiter, Saturn is still huge. You could fit 764 Earths inside of Saturn.

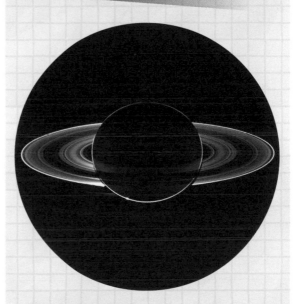

> A view we'll never see from Earth: this is backlit Saturn as seen by the Cassini spacecraft when it was in Saturn's shadow on the other side of the planet from the Sun.

USE YOUR EYES

> A MESSENGER spacecraft image of Mercury.

MERCURY

Mercury, the closest planet to the Sun, looks like a fairly bright star in the sky, but is much dimmer than Venus or Jupiter. Mercury can be hard to observe. That's because we never see it in the middle of the night. In fact, because Mercury is always near the Sun in the sky, the only times we can see it are very soon after sunset or very soon before sunrise.

Mercury is the smallest planet. Like the Moon, it has essentially no atmosphere. It also has a very old surface covered in impact craters—bowl-shaped features caused by space rocks hitting it repeatedly over billions of years.

To know when and where to look for Mercury, you'll need to check the Internet, magazines, or astronomy software or apps. See the Resources section for more information.

> THAT'S SO COOL!

Despite being the closest planet to the Sun, Mercury has water ice in the bottom of bowl-shaped craters near its poles. The bottoms of those craters never see sunlight, and there is no atmosphere to spread heat around.

> A MESSENGER spacecraft image of a heavily cratered area on Mercury.

> A picture of the Full Moon.

THE MOON

As I am sure you've noticed, the Earth's Moon is the brightest natural object in the night sky. And, unlike all the stars and planets, the Moon is close enough that we see it as a disk, not just a point of light.

Why do we see only part of that disk lit up sometimes? Just like the Earth, half of the Moon is lit up by the Sun at any given time. That is daytime on the Moon. Just as on Earth, the part of the Moon in daytime changes. But as the Moon goes around the Earth, which takes about a month, we see different amounts of the lit, or daytime, part of the Moon. We call these Moon phases or lunar phases. (*Lunar* is the adjective used for things having to do with the Moon.)

Full Moon is when the Moon is on the opposite side of Earth from the Sun so we see all the lit/day side of the Moon. Quarter Moon, which is often incorrectly called Half Moon,

occurs when we can see only half the day side. Watch the Moon as days go by and notice the changing phases. Many calendars, websites, and apps can tell you not only the phase of the Moon, but also when it will rise or set on a given night.

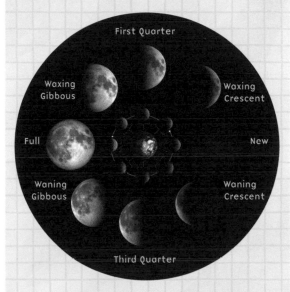

> *This diagram shows lunar phases. The center ring shows the Moon as it revolves around the Earth, as seen from above the North Pole. The Sun is imagined to be out of the picture far to the right. The outer ring shows what we see on the Earth during each corresponding part of the Moon's orbit.*

Continued on page 69

Continued from page 67

With just your eyes, try to notice the Moon's phases and see its bright and dark areas. The dark areas are called Maria (the singular is Mare) from the Latin word for "seas" because people used to think the dark areas were oceans. We now know they are composed of dark volcanic rocks. The brighter areas are called the Highlands because they are mountainous regions that are higher than the Maria. Though the Moon's entire surface is billions of years old, the Highlands are older than the Maria. With a telescope, you can see many more details on the Moon (page 129).

> THAT'S SO COOL!

The same side of the Moon always faces toward the Earth. We refer to that side as the Near Side. Earth's gravity and related tidal effects cause this.

> *The Moon is the only place besides Earth that humans have walked. This picture shows Apollo 15 astronaut Dave Scott on the Moon in 1971.*

USE YOUR EYES

> A picture of the sky showing some of the Milky Way. Within the Milky Way stripe, the camera's long exposure time highlights not only areas of increased brightness due to more stars but also darker regions where interstellar dust blocks light from distant stars. Your eyes are more likely to notice the increased fuzzy brightness of the Milky Way than the dark areas.

THE MILKY WAY GALAXY

We live in a galaxy called the Milky Way. The Milky Way is mostly flat. Imagine the Milky Way as a giant hamburger patty, but made up of stars. Now imagine you are inside the patty—not at the center, but about halfway to the edge. You look around. You see lots of stars in a broad stripe across where you look. That's where you are looking within the patty. When you look up or down, you don't see as many stars.

You probably won't notice this stripe we call the Milky Way if you are in a city. But if you're at a dark site, the Milky Way will be quite obvious.

Our galaxy is called the Milky Way because it looks milky—it has a fuzzy white brightness. And, no, it wasn't named after a candy bar; the candy bar was named after our galaxy!

> THAT'S SO COOL!

The Milky Way Galaxy has about 200 billion stars in it and is truly enormous. It is 100,000 light years across, meaning it takes light 100,000 years to cross the galaxy.

> A picture of a portion of the Milky Way taken with a camera. The information in the caption on the opposite page applies to this image as well.

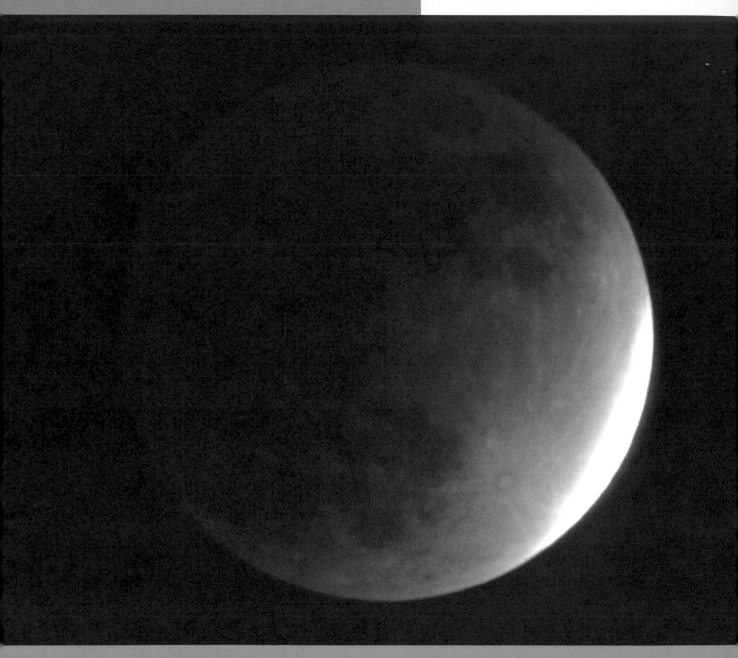

> An image of the Moon when almost totally eclipsed—in other words, when it's almost completely in Earth's shadow.

LUNAR ECLIPSE

A *total* **LUNAR ECLIPSE** occurs when the Moon completely enters the darkest part of the Earth's shadow, and a *partial* lunar eclipse occurs when the Moon moves only partly into the darkest part of the shadow.

A total lunar eclipse will be visible from where you live only every few years on average. When one does occur, everyone on the night side of Earth can see it. You can watch the Earth's shadow gradually darken the Moon, starting when the Moon just enters into the shadow. During a total eclipse, about an hour later, the whole Moon will be very dark. Then eventually it will leave the shadow.

Unlike solar eclipses (page 75) that are dangerous to look at with your eyes, lunar eclipses are perfectly safe. See the Resources section to learn how to find out when the next lunar eclipse will occur in your area.

> THAT'S SO COOL!

Lunar eclipses often make the Moon look red. This is because red light can pass through the edges of Earth's atmosphere and get bent toward the Moon. Other colors of light don't make it all the way through the atmosphere. This is the same reason sunsets appear red.

> An image of a total lunar eclipse.

USE YOUR EYES

73

> A picture of a total solar eclipse. The patterns around the Moon-blocked Sun are part of the Sun's very upper atmosphere called the corona. The orange areas are bright features extending far out from the "surface" of the Sun and are called prominences. **WARNING: Don't look directly at the Sun, even during the partial phases of a solar eclipse. The Sun will still be so bright it can cause blindness.**

SOLAR ECLIPSE

A **SOLAR ECLIPSE** occurs when the Moon's shadow crosses the Earth.

In a *total* solar eclipse, the Sun is completely blocked by the Moon. In a *partial* solar eclipse, the Sun is only partially blocked. Unlike lunar eclipses that are visible from a very large area, solar eclipses—particularly total eclipses—are much more localized. Unless you are very, very lucky, you will have to travel to see a total solar eclipse.

Partial solar eclipses cover a broader area but are still rare in any given location. The safest way to view a partial solar eclipse is to put a pinhole in a piece of cardboard, then stand with your back to the Sun. Hold the cardboard in the sunlight and use it to project an image of the Sun on the ground or onto a piece of paper. You'll see a bright circle that looks like it has a bite taken out of it. The "bite" is the part of the Moon that is

in front of the Sun. You can find out how to get information on when and where future solar eclipses will occur in the Resources section of this book.

> ## > THAT'S SO COOL!
> During a total solar eclipse, the Moon totally blocks the Sun for only about 1 to 6 minutes, depending on the eclipse.

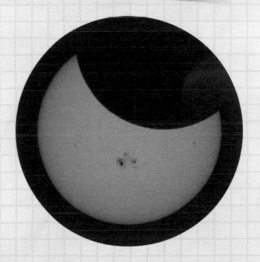

> A partial solar eclipse using a special safety filter. The curve of the Moon can easily be seen. The dark spots in the middle are called sun spots.

> An image of meteors (the streaks of light) captured in an hour-long camera exposure during a meteor shower.

METEOR SHOWERS

Meteors are streaks of light in the sky caused by space stuff burning up as it hits the upper atmosphere of the Earth at very high speeds. That space stuff usually consists of small dust and sand-sized dirt and rocks. Even these small things can cause streaks of light you can see from the ground at night. The bigger the dirt that hits, the brighter the light.

Any night of the year, if you watch the sky from a dark site, you may see 10 or so meteors per hour. There are also "meteor showers" that occur when Earth passes through the debris (stuff) left by a **COMET** sometime in the past. The next year, Earth will pass through the debris again on about the same date.

Two of the best meteor showers of the year are the Perseids, which peak around August 12 or 13, and the Geminids, which peak near December 13 or 14. During those showers, you can see 60 to 100 meteors per hour from a dark site. (From a bright city or when there is a Full Moon, you will see fewer.) All you need to watch meteors are your eyes, a cloudless night, and patience. Go out, get comfortable, and stare at the sky. See the Resources section to find out where you can learn about all the meteor showers of the year.

> THAT'S SO COOL!

Meteor showers are named after the constellation where the meteors appear to begin, so Geminid meteors all seem to come from a point in the constellation Gemini.

> A 2010 picture of the International Space Station taken from the Space Shuttle Atlantis during the STS-132 mission.

INTERNATIONAL SPACE STATION

The International Space Station (ISS) looks like an extremely bright star moving across the sky. It can be as bright as Venus. It looks like a plane but has no blinking or colored lights. What we are seeing is sunlight reflecting off the space station. The only time we can see it is when the ISS is in sunlight and we on the Earth's surface are in darkness, which usually occurs in the first 2 or 3 hours after sunset or the 2 or 3 hours just before dawn.

The ISS is a science laboratory in space. It orbits about 200 miles (about 400 kilometers) above the surface of the Earth. There have been people on the ISS since the year 2000. Each person generally spends a few months onboard. There are usually six people on the ISS at a time,

so when you see it flying over, think about the people who are living and working up there.

To know when and where to look for the ISS, you need predictions of the timing for your city or a nearby city. See the Resources section to find out where you can get these predictions. You can also see other satellites orbiting the Earth—there are websites and apps that predict those as well—but the ISS is usually the brightest, so it's the best satellite to start with.

> ## THAT'S SO COOL!

The International Space Station is about the size of a football field (including its large solar panels and numerous laboratory modules).

> CHAPTER 3

BEST WITH BINOCULARS

inoculars can add to the sky-viewing fun. They collect more light than your eyes do, allowing you to see dim objects that you can't see with just your eyes. Binoculars also magnify objects, which makes the objects look bigger. The result is that you'll be able to see more details. Telescopes, which we'll talk about in the next chapter, do these things as well and in some ways do them better. But binoculars have at least four advantages over telescopes:

1. Binoculars are usually cheaper.

2. Binoculars are much easier to use.

3. Binoculars are usually smaller and easier to carry with you.

4. Binoculars have a wider field of view so you'll see more of the sky at any one time. For some objects, like star clusters, a telescope may show only part of what you're trying to look at; binoculars will show it all.

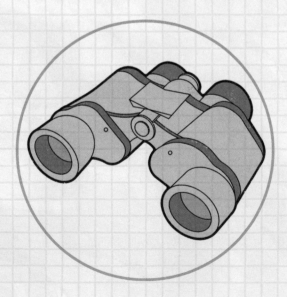

WHAT THE WEIRD BINOCULARS NUMBERS MEAN

Almost any binoculars will improve the detail you can see looking at the sky, but of course some are better than others. If you or your family is going to buy binoculars, I suggest you read some information online about buying binoculars for astronomical viewing. Whether you are buying them, borrowing them, or digging them out of the back of a closet, here is a brief overview of the basic differences between binoculars.

Binoculars are often described by two numbers. Usually written near an eye-piece will be numbers like 10 x 50, 8 x 40, or something similar. The first number is the **MAGNIFICATION**, which you can think of as how much bigger, or closer, an object will appear compared with viewing it with just your eyes. Bigger numbers magnify things more. The disadvantage to very big numbers (say 15 or 20) is that your field of view, or how much sky you can see, gets smaller. It also becomes harder to hold the binoculars still enough to keep the object you are looking at in sight.

The second number is the size of the big lenses on the front of the binoc-ulars. More precisely, it is the diameter of one of those lenses measured in millimeters. The bigger that number is, the more light you collect, which is very important in astronomy. However, if the number gets too big, then the binocu-lars get so heavy that it is hard to hold them still. Unless you are going to mount the binoculars on a tripod, you probably don't want to go above 50, and you might want 40 or 30 depending on how old you are and how much weight you can easily hold. It is more important to be comfortable holding your binoculars than it is to have big powerful binoculars (which you probably won't use because you can't hold them still).

SET THE STAGE

To observe with binoculars, you should do all the things we discussed in chapter 1 for observing using just your eyes, particularly adjusting your eyes to the dark.

One of the biggest challenges with binoculars is holding them mostly still while you are observing. You can sit in a chair and that can help. Some binoculars can also be connected to a camera tripod using an adapter. But even if you just hold them, you can often look at something for a short time and still get a lot out of what you are seeing.

You'll need to make at least two adjustments to the binoculars. First, "bend" them so the two eyepieces are exactly as far apart as your eyes. Second, adjust the focus using the wheel or lever in the middle of the binoculars until stars look like points—in other words, small dots. If one eye is focused and the other isn't, one of the eyepieces usually rotates to accommodate that eye.

THE BINOCULAR BIG 10

You can have fun looking at any part of the night sky with binoculars, but I've chosen to highlight 10 objects because they are either hard or impossible to see with just your eyes, or because binoculars are particularly good to view them with. These objects include:

> Star clusters (large groups of stars near each other in the sky and in space)
> Planets and their moons
> Nebulae (gas and dust usually left over from a star explosion)
> A galaxy (a group of billions of distant stars)
> Comets (big dirty snowballs with tails, kind of like my dogs, well, except for the snowballs part)

The objects in this chapter are organized in the same way as the objects in the last chapter.

[ORION]

Orion Nebula >

THE ORION NEBULA (M42)

Within the constellation Orion (page 27), there appears to be a sword made of three dimmer stars coming down from the belt. The middle star in the sword is actually the Orion Nebula, which you may be able to see even with just your eyes as a fuzzy patch. When you look with binoculars, you definitely should be able to see the fuzzy area. It is actually a gigantic (24 **LIGHT YEARS** across) cloud of dust and gas more than 1,300 light years away from us.

Though pictures often show colors in the nebula, your night-adjusted eyes may or may not be able to detect any color.

> ## > THAT'S SO COOL!
> Hundreds of stars are forming out of the dust and gas of the Orion Nebula. It is the closest star-forming region to Earth.

> A Hubble Space Telescope image of the Orion Nebula.

Betelgeuse

[TAURUS]

Aldebaran >

Rigel

THE HYADES STAR CLUSTER

The Hyades is an open cluster (a group of up to a few thousand stars together in a space that is rather spread out compared with a globular cluster) in Taurus. A few of the stars are visible with just your eyes, but many more will be visible with binoculars. The Hyades fill in the face of the bull Taurus.

The Hyades are right next to the bright star Aldebaran. Aldebaran is not part of the Hyades cluster—it is much closer to the Earth than the stars in the cluster. But Aldebaran makes it easy to locate the Hyades. So, to find the Hyades, look next to Aldebaran (page 31), which can be found by drawing a line through Orion's Belt and following it a bit more than 20 degrees (two fist widths at arm's length).

> ## THAT'S SO COOL!
> The Hyades is the closest open star cluster to Earth, at about 150 light years away.

> An image of the Hyades star cluster as taken with a telephoto lens. The bright star is Aldebaran, not actually part of the cluster, but many of the other stars are.

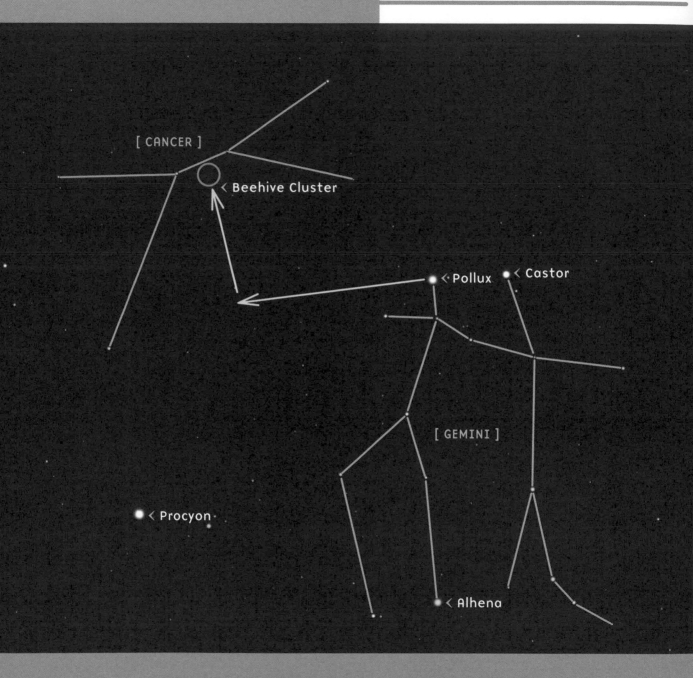

[CANCER]

< Beehive Cluster

< Pollux   < Castor

[GEMINI]

< Procyon

< Alhena

THE BEEHIVE CLUSTER (M44) IN CANCER

The Beehive Cluster is an open cluster in the middle of the constellation Cancer, "the Crab." With just your eyes from a dark site, the Beehive Cluster looks like a fuzzy patch. Binoculars will show lots of stars in it.

Some people think the stars look like bees swarming when they look through binoculars or a telescope. I think they look like popcorn popping, but that may just be because I'm hungry.

Cancer is between Leo (page 41) and Gemini (page 35). It is made up of rather dim stars, so it can be a little hard to identify. If you can find Cancer, then you'll find the Beehive Cluster just below the middle of a line connecting the two central stars of Cancer. Or you can use the bright stars Castor and Pollux of Gemini (perhaps combined with Leo) to find the cluster: draw a line from Castor to Pollux. Continue that line about three times farther, and then make a right turn and head up until you see the Beehive Cluster.

> ## THAT'S SO COOL!
The Beehive Cluster consists of about 1,000 stars. You'll see only some of them.

> A camera image of part of the Beehive Cluster.

BEST WITH BINOCULARS

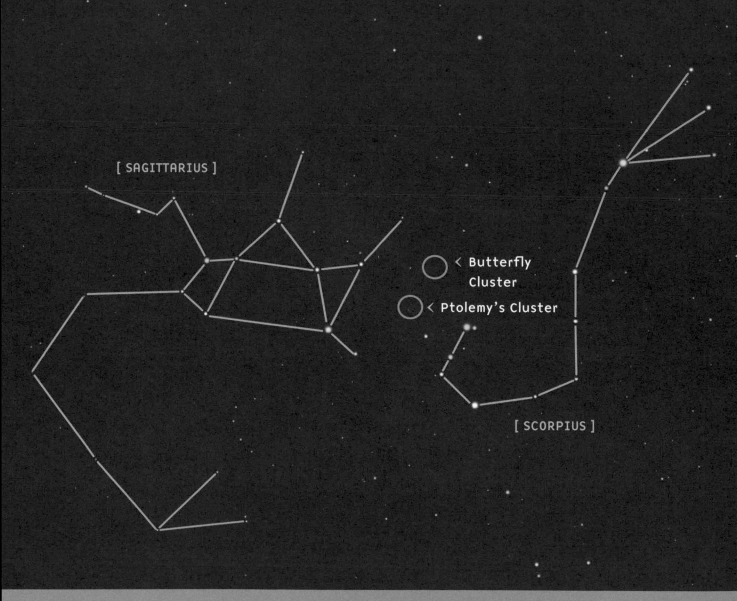

[SAGITTARIUS]

< Butterfly
Cluster

< Ptolemy's Cluster

[SCORPIUS]

PTOLEMY'S CLUSTER (M7) AND THE BUTTERFLY CLUSTER (M6)

Ptolemy's Cluster and the Butterfly Cluster are two open star clusters near the constellation Scorpius (page 47). Ptolemy's Cluster is the brighter of the two and can be seen as a fuzzy patch with just your eyes from a dark site, but with binoculars you should be able to make out individual stars in the cluster and be able to see it from brighter sites.

These two clusters can be found low in the Southern sky during the Summer. To find Ptolemy's Cluster, follow Scorpius's tail, which is shaped like a "J," around to the two stars next to each other that represent the scorpion's stinger. Look to the left of these stars to find Ptolemy's Cluster.

Look a little higher up to find the fainter Butterfly Cluster, said to look like a butterfly. What do you think it looks like?

> ## THAT'S SO COOL!
Ptolemy's Cluster covers an area more than twice as wide as the Full Moon.

> A picture of Ptolemy's Cluster (M7).

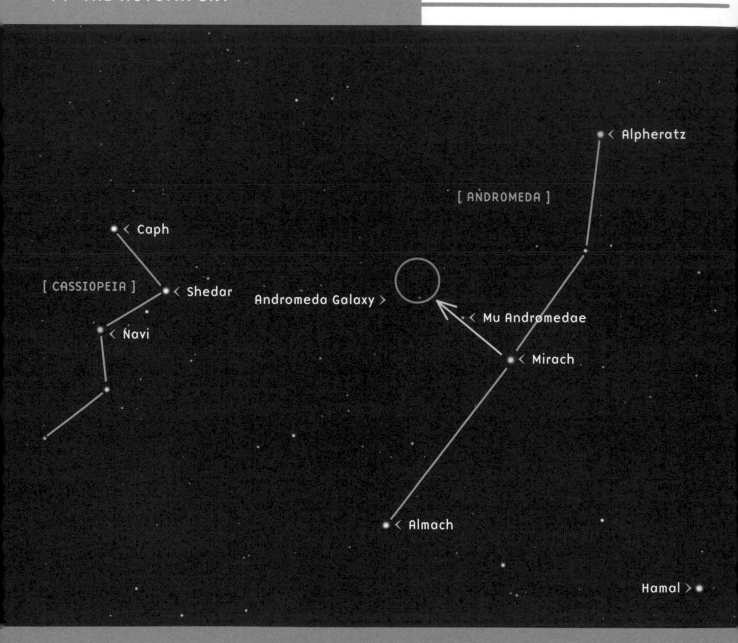

[ANDROMEDA]

< Alpheratz

< Caph

[CASSIOPEIA]

< Shedar

Andromeda Galaxy >

< Mu Andromedae

< Navi

< Mirach

< Almach

Hamal >

> *The Andromeda Galaxy isn't too exciting to see until you remember you are seeing light from a trillion stars, light that has been traveling through space for more than two million years to get to your eyes!*

THE ANDROMEDA GALAXY (M31)

The Andromeda Galaxy is the closest large galaxy to us in the Milky Way Galaxy (page 71). It is the farthest object you can see with just your eyes at 2.5 million light years away and contains about one trillion stars. You can see it with just your eyes in a dark sky, but you can see it more easily with binoculars.

To locate it, find the constellation Andromeda (page 53) first. You can start at the Big Dipper (page 19), follow the line from its stars Merak and Dubhe to Polaris, then continue on the line to the star Caph in Cassiopeia. One more similar length jump on the line will bring you to Andromeda's "head" star, Alpheratz. Follow down Andromeda until you reach the hip stars of Andromeda: brighter Mirach and dimmer Mu Andromedae. Draw a line from Mirach to Mu Andromedae. Then continue along that line the same distance again and you'll reach the Andromeda Galaxy. It will look like a long fuzzy patch!

> ## THAT'S SO COOL!
The Andromeda Galaxy will merge with our Milky Way Galaxy, forming a new combined galaxy, about 4.5 billion years from now.

> *A telescopic picture of the Andromeda Galaxy.*

Caph >

[CASSIOPEIA]

Navi >

< Ruchbah

< Double Cluster

THE DOUBLE CLUSTER

The appropriately named Double Cluster consists of two open star clusters (collections of stars named NGC 869 and NGC 884) that appear close together in the sky. From a very dark site, they might be visible with just your eyes, but using binoculars will make them visible in most lighting conditions.

Though technically in the constellation Perseus, the Double Cluster is easiest to locate from Cassiopeia (page 23). If you imagine writing the Cassiopeia constellation as the letter "M," draw a line though the third and fourth stars (Navi and Ruchbah) and it will approximately guide you to the Double Cluster, as shown in the illustration to the left. Look for two collections of many tens of stars of similar brightness.

> ## > THAT'S SO COOL!
> The stars in both star clusters are very young by astronomy standards, though very old by human standards. They formed a little less than 13 million years ago. For comparison, the Sun is about 5 billion years old.

> A picture of the Double Cluster.

> A picture of Uranus taken by the Voyager 2 spacecraft, the only spacecraft to have flown by Uranus.

URANUS

Uranus is the seventh planet from the Sun. Sometimes it is visible with just your eyes in a very dark sky. But most of the time you'll need binoculars or a telescope. When viewed through binoculars, it will look like a star. You might be able to detect its blue-green color, but you might not. Through a large enough telescope, it may appear as a small disk, and you may be able to see its color.

Though much smaller than Jupiter and Saturn, Uranus is still much larger than Earth—63 Earths could fit inside it. It is just slightly larger than Neptune, the eighth planet from the Sun (page 135). More fun facts: Uranus is a giant planet with a thick atmosphere, it takes Uranus 84 Earth years to go around the Sun, and it has a set of 13 dim rings and at least 27 small moons.

To know when and where to look for Uranus, you'll need to check out the Internet, magazines, or astronomy software or apps. See the Resources section for more information.

> ## THAT'S SO COOL!
Uranus is tilted on its side compared with its orbit, meaning it appears to spin on its side.

> A 2006 image of Uranus taken by the Hubble Space Telescope. More cloud variations can be seen compared with the Voyager 2 image, because there was more cloud activity and slightly different wavelengths (colors).

> The above image of Jupiter and the Galilean Moons is not from one picture, but a combination of pictures of each of the objects taken by the Voyager 1 spacecraft. Sizes and distances are not to scale. From left to right: Io, Ganymede, Europa, Jupiter, and Callisto.

JUPITER'S
GALILEAN MOONS

Amazingly, with binoculars, you can see Jupiter's four largest moons: Io, Europa, Ganymede, and Callisto. They look like four stars that are much dimmer than Jupiter. They will appear approximately in a line. If one happens to be behind or in front of Jupiter, you may see only three on a particular night. The really cool thing is that you can watch them move from night to night as they go around Jupiter.

In 1610, the famous scientist Galileo was the first to observe these four moons and now the group is named after him: the Galilean moons or Galilean satellites. (Moons are also called natural satellites.) His observations were also the first evidence of objects moving around something other than Earth.

The Galilean moons are fascinating worlds themselves. Io is the most volcanically active body in the Solar System, Europa has an ocean deep under its icy surface, Ganymede is the largest moon in the Solar System, and Callisto has an old, cratered surface.

Jupiter has at least 79 moons, but all the others are much smaller and not visible with binoculars or small telescopes.

To know when and where to look for Jupiter and its moons, you'll need to check out the Internet, magazines, or astronomy software or apps. See the Resources section for more information.

> ## THAT'S SO COOL!
Ganymede, the largest moon in the Solar System, is bigger than the planet Mercury.

> A Cassini spacecraft image of Saturn, its rings seen edge on, the shadows of the rings on Saturn, and in the foreground, its largest moon, Titan.

TITAN
SATURN'S MOON

Saturn's largest moon, Titan, is visible with good sky conditions and binoculars. It will look like a star. From night to night you can watch it move.

Titan is the second-largest moon in the Solar System and is larger than the planet Mercury. It is the only moon in the Solar System to have a thick atmosphere—thicker than Earth's. The hazy clouds in its atmosphere would prevent you from seeing the surface even if you were in the Saturn system. Scientists have used other wavelengths of light (colors you can't see) such as infrared and radio waves to see through the atmosphere to the surface.

To know when and where to look for Saturn and Titan, you'll need to check out the Internet, magazines, or astronomy software or apps. You can even use these resources to predict where Titan will be relative to Saturn on the night you observe. See the Resources section for more information.

> **THAT'S SO COOL!**
> Titan has rainfall and liquid seas but they aren't made of water. Water is frozen that far from the Sun. The rain and seas are made of methane and ethane—what we call natural gas on Earth.

> *A mosaic of images of Titan as seen at infrared wavelengths that would be invisible to your eyes, but not to a special camera on the Cassini spacecraft. This camera sees through the cloudy haze to the moon's surface.*

> *An image of a comet, including its tail.*

COMETS

Comets are some of the best objects to observe with binoculars because they can cover a large area of the sky. Comets are dirty snowballs, or snowy dirtballs, that can be the size of a city. They spend most of their time in the outer Solar System, far beyond the orbit of Neptune.

The challenge with comets is we don't know where most of them are until they start coming closer to the Sun. As they grow closer to the Sun, their surface ice heats up and starts turning to gas. As this happens, dirt and gas are kicked off the comet, creating an area of gas and dust called the coma, which then is spread out by the effects of the Sun into a long tail.

Sometimes, you can see one or two comets with binoculars that will look like tiny fuzzy blobs. Every few years, a comet comes close enough to the Sun and to Earth that it will be visible with just your eyes and more

spectacular with binoculars. Some comets come back around regularly, like Halley's Comet (which comes to the inner Solar System every 86 years or so).

To know when and where to look for comets is tricky. Most nights there aren't any to see. Check websites like *Sky and Telescope* or *Astronomy* for articles about any visible comets. See the Resources section for more information.

> ## THAT'S SO COOL!

Unlike my dogs' tails, comet tails aren't always behind them. Comet tails always point away from the Sun because sunlight and what is called the solar wind come from the Sun and push out the comet tails. That means the tails are behind the comet when it is heading toward the Sun, but in front of the comet when it is heading away from the Sun.

> CHAPTER 4

STEP UP TO A TELESCOPE

Telescopes allow you to see even more detail in sky objects than binoculars or your eyes by collecting more light and magnifying images more (making the objects appear bigger). Telescopes are the devices most associated with astronomers, even though, as we have discussed, using just your eyes is the best way to first become familiar with astronomy. If you have a telescope, or are thinking of getting one, this chapter is for you. I'll give you some basic information about telescopes and buying them, and some information on how they work and how to use them. Then I'll introduce you to my top 10 objects to observe with a telescope.

TELESCOPE BASICS

If you want to buy a telescope, or just understand them better, it helps to start with some basics. So let's learn about types of telescopes and related equipment.

TYPES OF TELESCOPES

All amateur telescopes gather light (from a planet or galaxy, for example), then direct that light to an eyepiece where you can look at that light with your eye—and see the object. There are two basic ways to take the light from a big area (think of that as the front of the telescope) to a small area like your eye. When the telescope uses mirrors to do this, it is called a *reflecting* telescope, because it reflects light off curved mirrors. When the telescope uses lenses to do this, it is called a *refracting* telescope, because it refracts or bends light using lenses. Some telescopes use a combination of mirrors and lenses. These are called *compound* telescopes or, if you want to use a fancy word, *catadioptric* telescopes. To make things even more confusing, each basic type of telescope has different ways the mirrors or lenses can be laid out, and each way gets its own name, like Newtonian, Dobsonian, Schmidt–Cassegrain, or Super-Light-Bendy. Okay, I made up that last one. But the others and many more are real.

> A compound telescope.

> A reflecting telescope.

> A refracting telescope.

IMPORTANT STUFF TO GO WITH A TELESCOPE

MOUNTS. Telescopes require other things to go with them. One is a mount. That's what holds the telescope and allows you to point it in different directions. A mount also helps you hold the telescope steady. It is important to have a stable mount so the telescope doesn't shake when you're trying to look at objects in the sky. Some mounts are tripod-shaped and some have other shapes.

There are different kinds of mounts. Most are what are called altitude-azimuth mounts, which is a fancy way of saying they move up and down and side to side. The other main type of mount is called equatorial, which is a design that is particularly good for motorizing. Why would you want to motorize a mount? Because objects in the sky are always moving as the Earth rotates. Equatorial mounts with motorized capability can follow the objects as they move. But an equatorial mount is complicated to set up each time, and although following an object across the sky can be helpful, it is not necessary.

EYEPIECES. Another thing you need is at least one eyepiece. The eyepiece is the part of the telescope you look through and includes the final lens that the light passes through on the way to your eye. Some inexpensive telescopes have permanently attached eyepieces. But with many telescopes, you can change the eyepiece. A new telescope almost always comes with at least one eyepiece and sometimes has multiple. Eyepieces will adjust the magnification of your telescope setup. Although you may think you'll always want to use the eyepiece with the highest magnification, sometimes it is better to use lower magnification eyepieces that make it easier to find objects. Higher magnification has a narrower field of view and in less-than-perfect viewing conditions, higher magnification will not necessarily improve your view of the object.

FINDER SCOPES. Telescopes also include a finder scope or its equivalent. A finder scope is basically a small telescope attached to your big telescope. The two need to be lined up so they look at the same point in the distance. Because the big telescope sees only a tiny part of the sky, it's very hard to find what you're looking for in it. So you use the small finder scope to center on the object, and then you look through the big telescope to make minor changes to where you're looking.

GOTO TELESCOPES. More expensive telescopes often are computer-controlled (sometimes called GoTo) telescopes. If you set this scope up properly at the beginning of a night of observing, it will automatically go to the object you tell it you want to view. Pretty cool. It makes finding things easier, but requires you to first find certain bright stars to set up the telescope each time. It also takes away some of the fun of finding objects yourself through learning the night sky, as you've been doing with this book.

HOW TO BUY A TELESCOPE

If you and your family decide to buy a telescope, the previous information will help you know what you're looking at. Although they're fun, telescopes should not be considered "toys." Because telescopes often a cost a lot, and they last a long time if properly cared for, I recommend you research them before you buy.

Here are a few tips to get you started:

> Look online for telescope buying guides. See the Resources section for suggestions.

> If you can, contact a local astronomy club and find out when you can attend a star party they're having. There you can look through various types of telescopes and ask people about them. See the Resources section to learn how to find your local astronomy club.

> There is no single best telescope for everyone, just as there is no one best car or best bicycle for everyone. You need to decide what is best for you. For example, big telescopes collect more light but they're going to be heavier and more expensive.

> The aperture is the front end of the telescope. Telescopes give their aperture size in either inches or millimeters. In general, the bigger the aperture, the better. That's because bigger apertures mean the telescope will be able to collect more light. More light means you can see dimmer objects and see more detail in the objects you look at. Aperture size is usually the most important thing in determining what you will be able to see.

> Although magnification is important, a big aperture is more important. Beware of telescopes that emphasize their large magnification (for example, 600x). On smaller telescopes, very large magnification is useless because the image will become blurry. Also, all but perfect sky conditions will render extremely high magnification useless.

> Consider how important it is that your telescope is easy to carry and set up. A big, complex telescope isn't fun if you don't ever want to get it out and set it up or take it somewhere to view the night sky.

> You can always start small and then get a larger telescope later as you learn more. You'll be able to have fun seeing things even with a relatively small telescope.

> Consider buying a reputable telescope brand. See the Resources section at the back of this book for suggestions.

STEP UP TO A TELESCOPE

HOW TO USE A TELESCOPE

You need to know how a telescope works before you can make it work for you. The most important thing to do is to read the directions in the telescope manual. Different telescopes work differently, so you'll need to read the information specific to your telescope.

Here are some general things you'll want to do with your telescope:

> Identify ahead of time, using this book or other resources, objects you'd like to try to look at that are consistent with the season and time you'll be viewing the sky.
> Adjust your eyes to the dark and use other techniques discussed in chapter 1 (page 1).
> If you have more than one eyepiece, or have an adjustable eyepiece, use a low magnification at first for any object you're trying to view. That will make it easier to find what you're looking for.
> Point your telescope at some stars and adjust the focus until they appear as points of light or as small as you can get them.
> For each object you want to view, first look with just your eyes to find it or the area you expect it to be in.
> Point the finder scope or its equivalent at the object or place in the sky and center it.

> Look through the telescope and carefully adjust the position and focus if needed.

> Once the object is positioned and focused, do not touch the telescope while you're observing because you don't want to shake it. Consider putting your hands behind your back while you're looking through the eyepiece.

> For faint objects like galaxies, nebulae, and some star clusters, you may or may not be able to see them depending on sky conditions. Be patient and try again on another night if you don't see something the first time you look.

> Be safe and have fun!

THE TELESCOPE TOP 10

If you're fortunate enough to own or have access to a telescope, you can explore the treasures in the sky in more detail. Here are the top 10 objects—in all their glory—that I think deserve your telescopic attention.

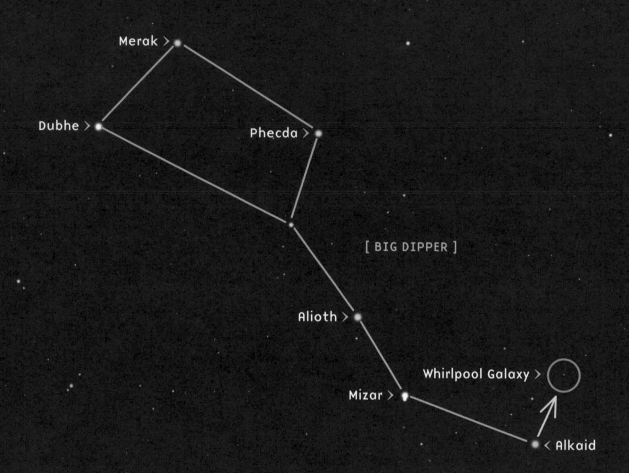

Merak >

Dubhe >

Phecda >

[BIG DIPPER]

Alioth >

Whirlpool Galaxy >

Mizar >

< Alkaid

THE WHIRLPOOL GALAXY (M51)

The Whirlpool Galaxy is a spiral, whirlpool-shaped galaxy, which is where it got its name. It also has a dwarf galaxy next to it called NGC 5195. Depending on sky conditions and the size and quality of your telescope, you may see the Whirlpool Galaxy as a fuzzy or cloudy patch, or roughly circular. With larger telescopes, you may even be able to see a little bit of its spiral nature or the dwarf galaxy.

To find the Whirlpool Galaxy, use the end star in the handle of the Big Dipper, known as Alkaid. The Whirlpool Galaxy will be 3 to 4 degrees from it on the opposite side of the Big Dipper from the North Star. If you are observing in the evening, look for the galaxy in the Spring and Summer because it will be higher above the horizon and easier to see.

> An image of the Whirlpool Galaxy, combining images from the Hubble Space Telescope and a ground-based telescope on Kitt Peak in Arizona.

STEP UP TO A TELESCOPE

117

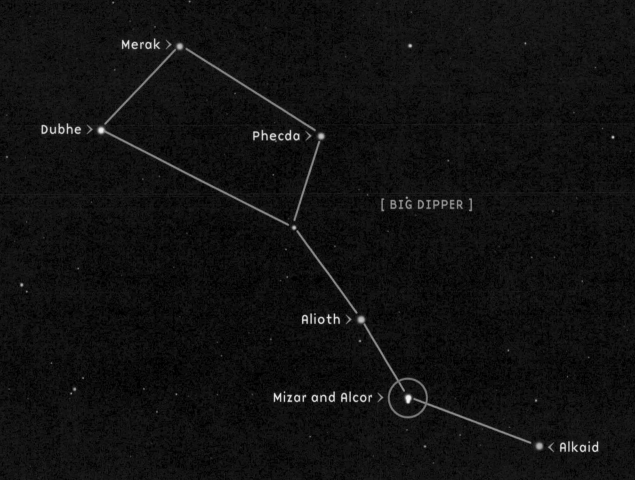

Merak >

Dubhe >

Phecda >

[BIG DIPPER]

Alioth >

Mizar and Alcor >

< Alkaid

MIZAR AND ALCOR
IN THE BIG DIPPER

Mizar and Alcor make up the center of the handle of the Big Dipper, so to find them just locate the Big Dipper (page 19) and look for the middle star in the handle. With your unaided eyes and good viewing conditions, you can probably see that the middle star of the Big Dipper is actually two stars: Mizar is the brighter one and Alcor is its dimmer companion.

Mizar is particularly interesting through a telescope because you will likely be able to see that Mizar is actually two stars, not just one.

> The above image is of Mizar (top) and Alcor. Note that through a telescope you also may be able to see that Mizar is a double star (not visible in this picture). The lines coming out of the stars are not real; they are effects of the telescope's internal parts.

STEP UP TO A TELESCOPE

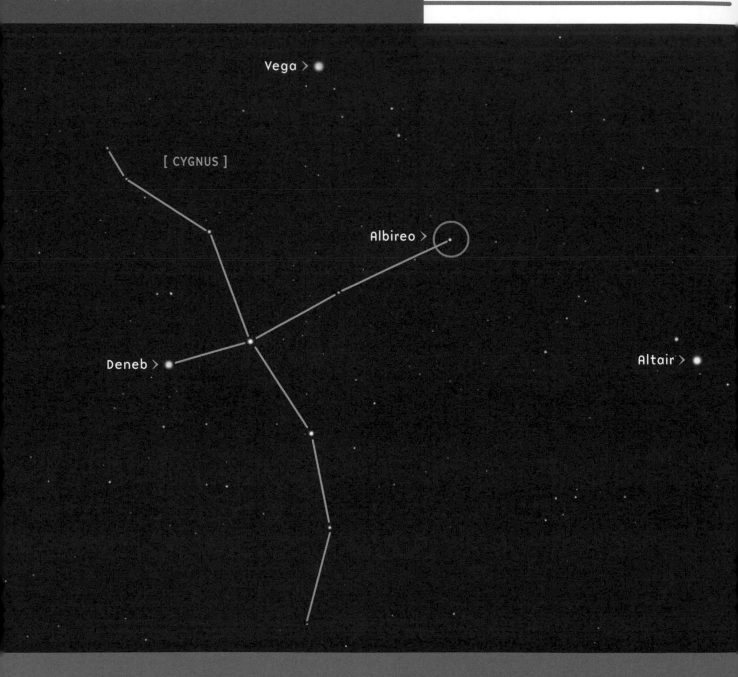

ALBIREO,
A DOUBLE STAR IN CYGNUS

Albireo is a beautiful **DOUBLE STAR** in Cygnus, the "Swan." It looks like one star to your unaided eyes, but a telescope reveals two stars of very different colors: a brighter yellow star and a dimmer blue star. It is easy to find Albireo. Find Cygnus (page 45) first. Albireo is the head of the swan or the base of the cross in the Northern Cross.

(page 45)

> ## THAT'S SO COOL!
> Albireo is sometimes called the "beak star" since it is at the head of Cygnus the Swan.

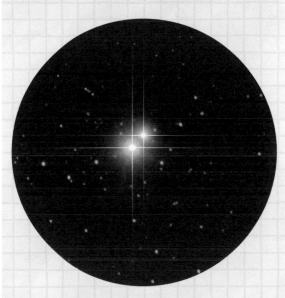

> A telescopic image of Albireo showing the two stars of different colors. The lines coming out of the stars are not real; they are effects of the telescope's internal parts.

STEP UP TO A TELESCOPE

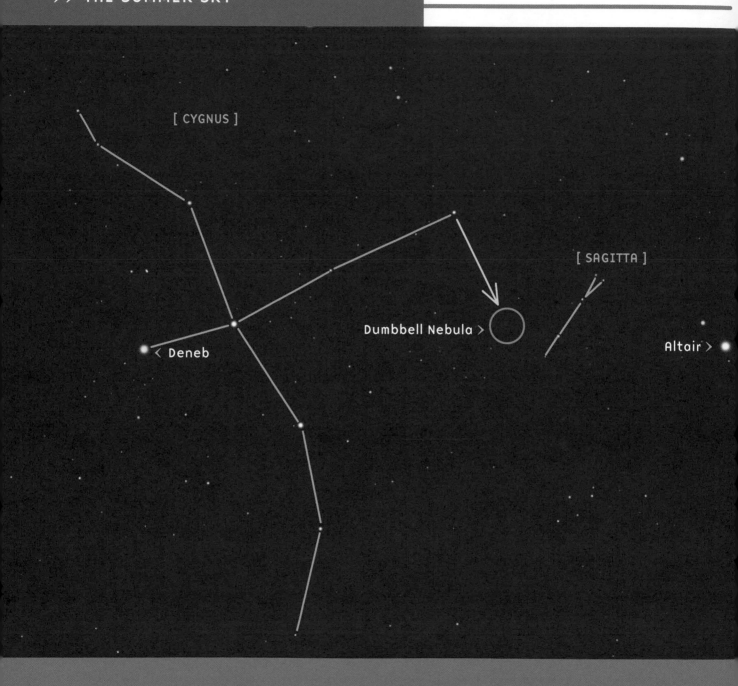

[CYGNUS]

[SAGITTA]

Dumbbell Nebula >

< Deneb

Altair >

THE DUMBBELL NEBULA (M27)

The Dumbbell Nebula is a nebula that will appear through a telescope like a small fuzzy patch. With a dark sky and/or a larger telescope and eyes adjusted to the dark, you may be able to see a dumbbell or bow-tie shape, and you may detect some color in it.

The Dumbbell Nebula is a **PLANETARY NEBULA**. To find it, start by finding the Summer Triangle (page 43). The nebula is a little more than halfway along a line between the bright stars Deneb and Altair of the Summer Triangle. You can also use Cygnus (page 45) and the star Albireo to work your way to the Dumbbell Nebula. Move down the cross to Albireo, then make a right-angled right turn. Go until you hit the line between Deneb and Altair and look for the nebula. You can also use the stars of the small constellation Sagitta to get close to the nebula.

> **THAT'S SO COOL!**
The Dumbbell Nebula was the first planetary nebula to be discovered.

> *The Dumbbell Nebula as imaged by the Spitzer Space Telescope in infrared light.*

STEP UP TO A TELESCOPE

123

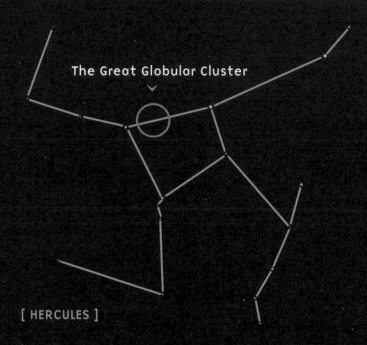

The Great Globular Cluster

[HERCULES]

< Vega

THE GREAT GLOBULAR CLUSTER (M13)

The Great Globular Cluster, also known as the Great Star Cluster or the Hercules Globular Cluster (because it is in the constellation Hercules), is one of the easiest-to-see globular clusters from Northern latitudes.

With a small telescope, this cluster will look like a small ball of light with the center brighter than the outside. A larger telescope will start to reveal lots and lots of stars looking like they are on top of a fuzzy background.

To locate this star cluster, start by finding the Summer Triangle (page 43) and the bright star Vega. From there, find the asterism that looks kind of like a messy square in the fairly dim constellation Hercules. That asterism is called the Keystone. The Great Globular Cluster is about one-third of the way along a line between the two stars making up the far side of the square from Vega.

> ## THAT'S SO COOL!
> Stars in globular clusters are some of the oldest in the galaxy, at about 10 billion years old.

> An image of the core of the Great Globular Cluster taken with the Hubble Space Telescope.

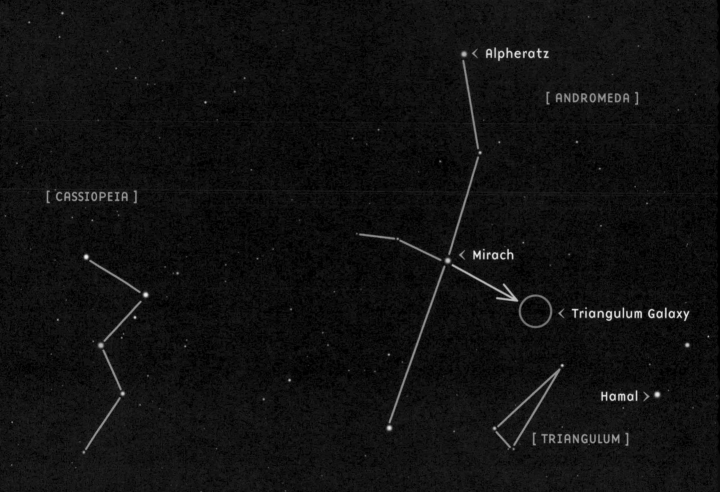

< Alpheratz

[ANDROMEDA]

[CASSIOPEIA]

< Mirach

< Triangulum Galaxy

Hamal >

[TRIANGULUM]

THE TRIANGULUM GALAXY (M33)

The Triangulum Galaxy will be challenging to see if you don't have dark skies, but rewarding to see if you do. It is a spiral galaxy, but does not have a bright center like the Andromeda Galaxy (page 95), making it harder to be sure you are seeing it. It covers a significant area, so try using a low-magnification eyepiece. With dark skies, you may be able to distinguish two of its spiral "arms."

To find the Triangulum Galaxy, start by finding the constellation Andromeda (page 53). If you have found the Andromeda Galaxy, the Triangulum Galaxy is about the same distance in the opposite direction from the star Mirach in Andromeda. You can also use the small Triangulum constellation to help you.

> An image of the Triangulum Galaxy taken by the WISE space telescope using infrared light, so it looks different from what is seen with your eyes. In this picture, the bluish colors are mostly stars and the reds and greens are mostly dust.

STEP UP TO A TELESCOPE

127

> *An image of the Moon's surface from lunar orbit showing many impact craters.*

THE MOON'S CRATERS AND MOUNTAINS

The Moon can be a cool target in binoculars and a great target in a telescope. With a telescope, you will be able to easily see many impact craters, the places where asteroids (space rocks) hit the Moon in the distant past and left bowl-shaped holes. You can also see mountains on the Moon.

The easiest way to see craters and mountains is to point your telescope near the line separating the very bright (daytime) part of the Moon from the very dark (nighttime) part of the Moon. That line is called the terminator. Near the terminator, shadows will be longer and that will help you see differences in elevation.

Note: there will be no terminator visible during Full Moon, but there will be in all other phases. How many craters can you see? I'm guessing a lot.

When the Moon is up, it's easy to find because it's so bright. You can find when the Moon will rise and set for your location on the Internet, in a newspaper, or with astronomy software or apps. Don't plan to look at dim sky objects right after looking at the Moon. The Moon is bright enough in a telescope that it will mess up your dark-adapted night vision.

> **THAT'S SO COOL!**
Thirty Earths would fit between the Earth and the Moon.

> A Cassini spacecraft image of Saturn and its rings.

SATURN'S RINGS

Saturn is famous for having an elaborate set of rings around it. With a small telescope, you can not only see Saturn (page 63) and its moon Titan (page 103), but you can also actually see the rings, though Saturn and the rings may look small.

For many people, their first time seeing the rings is one of the most amazing and memorable experiences in astronomy. Incredibly, you can see Saturn's famous rings even though they are one billion miles (one and a half billion kilometers) away.

> THAT'S SO COOL!

Saturn's rings are made of "slightly dirty snowballs," pieces of water ice mixed with some dust. There are billions of them ranging from the size of dust to the size of houses.

> An image from the Cassini spacecraft of part of Saturn's rings, made up of dirty snowballs ranging in size from tiny to huge.

> A Hubble Space Telescope image of Jupiter clearly showing its cloud bands (stripes) and the Great Red Spot.

JUPITER'S CLOUDS

With a telescope, not only can you see the Galilean moons of Jupiter (page 101), but you can also start to make out Jupiter's different-colored cloud stripes. Usually, you can make out one darker reddish stripe in the top half of Jupiter and one darker reddish stripe in the bottom half, with lighter areas between and above and below. Larger telescopes may see more stripes or may even see the Great Red Spot if it is facing Earth at the time.

To know when and where to look for Jupiter, you'll need to check out the Internet, magazines, or astronomy software or apps. See the Resources section for more information.

> A Cassini spacecraft view of Jupiter, including its cloud bands and the Great Red Spot.

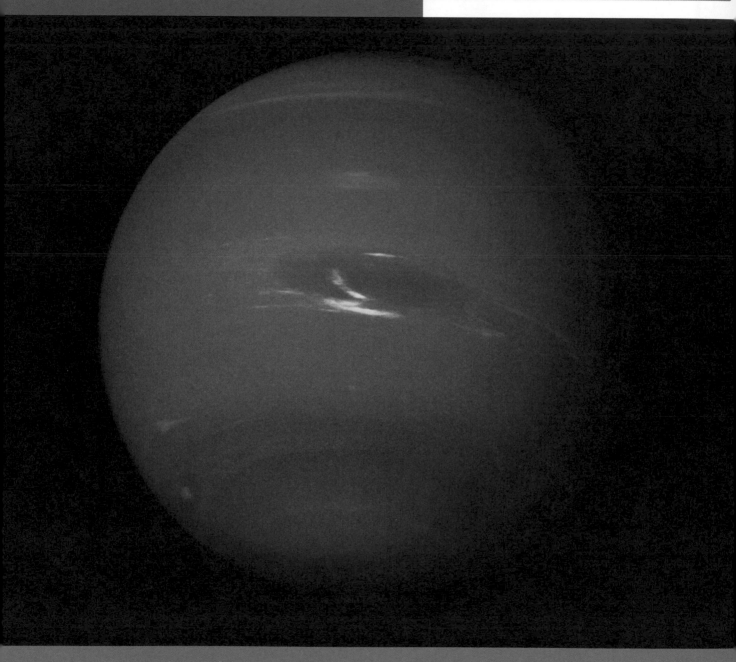

> A Voyager 2 spacecraft image of Neptune, including the Great Dark Spot, a storm that has gone away since Voyager 2 flew by in 1989.

NEPTUNE AND TRITON

Neptune is the eighth planet from the Sun. Even through a telescope, it will likely appear as a dot, or you may be able to distinguish it as a small disk. You also may be able to see its blue color.

Neptune is a giant planet with a thick atmosphere and is similar in size to Uranus (page 99). With an 8-inch or larger telescope, you may be able to see Neptune's largest moon, Triton, appearing as a dot.

To know when and where to look for Neptune, you'll need to check out the Internet, magazines, or astronomy software or apps. See the Resources section for more information.

> ## THAT'S SO COOL!
Neptune has the fastest winds of any planet in the Solar System, with winds as high as 1,300 miles per hour (2,100 kilometers per hour).

> A Voyager 2 picture of Triton, showing its weird icy terrains.

> CHAPTER 5

KEEP EXPLORING

The universe is amazing and you have just begun to explore and learn about it. In this book, I have shared with you 50 of the easiest and most interesting things to observe in the night sky. That is just the beginning! There are 88 constellations, counting both hemispheres. And with just your eyes, there are more than 2,000 stars to see every night from a dark site. There is a huge number of deep-sky objects like galaxies, nebulae, and star clusters visible with binoculars and telescopes. I hope you will take what you have learned from this book, gather more information, and keep going out, looking up, learning, and having fun!

THE NEXT STEPS

Consider taking some of these next steps in astronomy:

> Learn more about space and get involved with others who share your interest and enthusiasm.
> Use the resources (websites, magazines, videos, etc.) you find in the Resources section of this book or that you find on your own to:
  - discover other things you can look for in the night sky, including objects that are more difficult to see
  - learn when planets, satellites, eclipses, and comets are visible
  - find groups of other people who share your interest in astronomy (for example, amateur astronomy clubs and The Planetary Society)
  - watch fun and educational videos (see the Resources section for links)
> Find out what large professional telescopes and planetary spacecraft are showing us and teaching us about objects you can see and ones you can't.

> Learn more about the objects you are viewing.
> Follow the author and/or other space and astronomy accounts on social media.
> Explore more advanced viewing equipment like (better) binoculars and (better) telescopes.
> Consider whether some day you want to be a professional astronomer or planetary scientist, or would like another career in the space field, which could range from engineering to teaching. If so, explore those careers; find out what engineers, teachers, and others do and how to become one.
> Try to observe the five tough objects in the next section.

AIM HIGH

Challenge yourself and see if you can observe these five more advanced targets. They can be difficult to find. All but the **VARIABLE STAR** Algol will require a telescope and a dark sky (with probably no light from the Moon). Algol will require repeated observations.

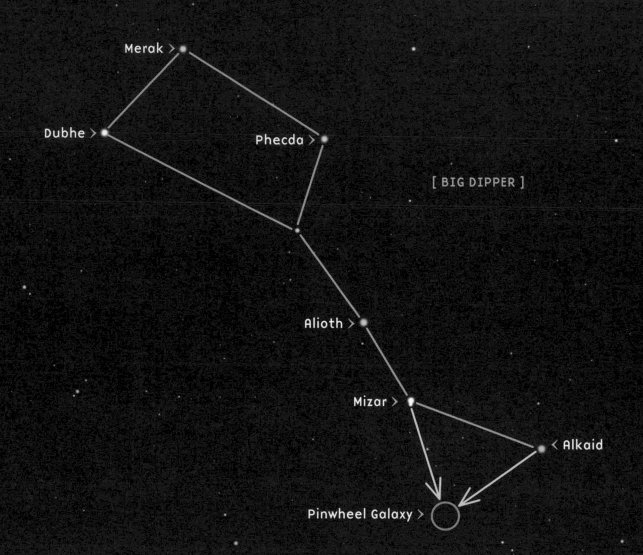

[BIG DIPPER]

THE PINWHEEL GALAXY (M101)

The Pinwheel Galaxy is a spiral galaxy that is dim enough to require dark skies and a medium-sized telescope. It will likely appear as a fuzzy or cloudy patch. With larger telescopes, you may even be able to see a little bit of its spiral.

To find the Pinwheel Galaxy, you can use the two stars at the end of the handle of the Big Dipper, Mizar and Alkaid. The Whirlpool Galaxy will be 3 to 4 degrees from both on the same side of the dipper as Polaris, forming a triangle with all three sides being about the same length at a little more than 5 degrees. If you are observing in the evening, looking for it in the Spring and Summer will be easiest because it will be higher above the horizon.

> **THAT'S SO COOL!**
The Pinwheel Galaxy is so far away that the light you are seeing left its stars 21 million years ago.

> The Pinwheel Galaxy in an image that combines pictures from three space telescopes: Spitzer (infrared light), Hubble (visible), and Chandra (X-ray).

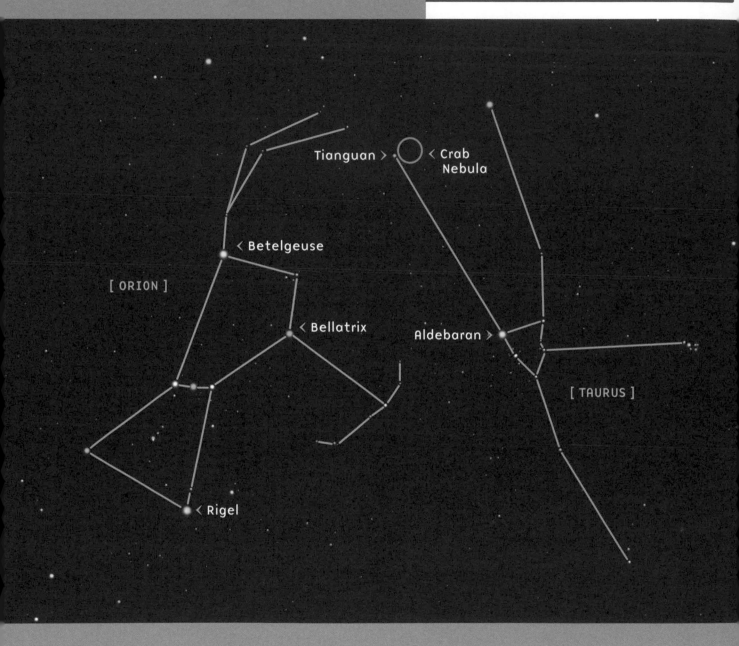

Tianguan >

< Crab Nebula

< Betelgeuse

[ORION]

< Bellatrix

Aldebaran >

[TAURUS]

< Rigel

> *This picture of the Crab Nebula (opposite page) was made by combining several pictures taken by the Hubble Space Telescope. With a small telescope, you will see it as a fuzzy smudge.*

THE CRAB NEBULA
(M1)

The Crab Nebula will appear as a dim, oval-shaped patch of light with an amateur telescope. Make sure you look for it when the Moon is not up, since any moonlight in the sky will make it very hard to find. Ideally, look for it from a dark site.

To locate it, use Orion's Belt to find the bright star Aldebaran (page 31) in Taurus. Then follow a line out to the somewhat bright star Tianguan at the end of the left (as you are seeing it) horn of Taurus. Move into the space between the horns just a little more than a degree.

The Crab Nebula is a **SUPERNOVA REMNANT**, meaning it consists of the gas and dust left over from the **SUPERNOVA** explosion of a huge star at the end of its life. The brightness from a supernova explosion at the end of a huge star's life can cause the sudden appearance of a new bright star in the sky that then fades over weeks and months.

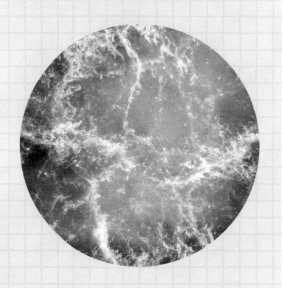

Vega >

[LYRA]

< Sheliak

< Ring Nebula

< Sulafat

THE RING NEBULA
(M57)

The Ring Nebula is well known, not surprisingly, for its ring shape. Depending on sky conditions and the size of the telescope, it can be mistaken for a star because it is pretty small. But even with a 3-inch or 4-inch telescope, you may see it as a small, cloudy circular shape. With a larger telescope and eyes adjusted to the dark, you may be able to see the ring shape. The Ring Nebula is a planetary nebula.

Though it can be a tough object to see well, the directions for finding it are fairly easy. Find bright Vega, part of the Summer Triangle (page 43). Vega is part of the constellation Lyra. The two fairly bright end stars of Lyra, Sheliak and Sulafat, can be found about halfway between Vega and Albireo (page 121). Look for the Ring Nebula a little less than halfway between Sheliak and Sulafat.

> THAT'S SO COOL!

There is a small, very hot star at the center of the Ring Nebula. Though too dim to see with most amateur telescopes, this star created the nebula and it provides the energy to make the gas cloud glow.

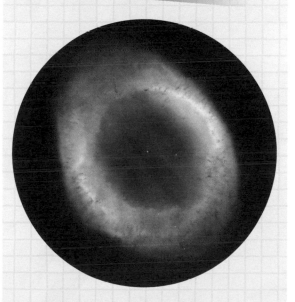

> A Hubble Space Telescope image of the Ring Nebula.

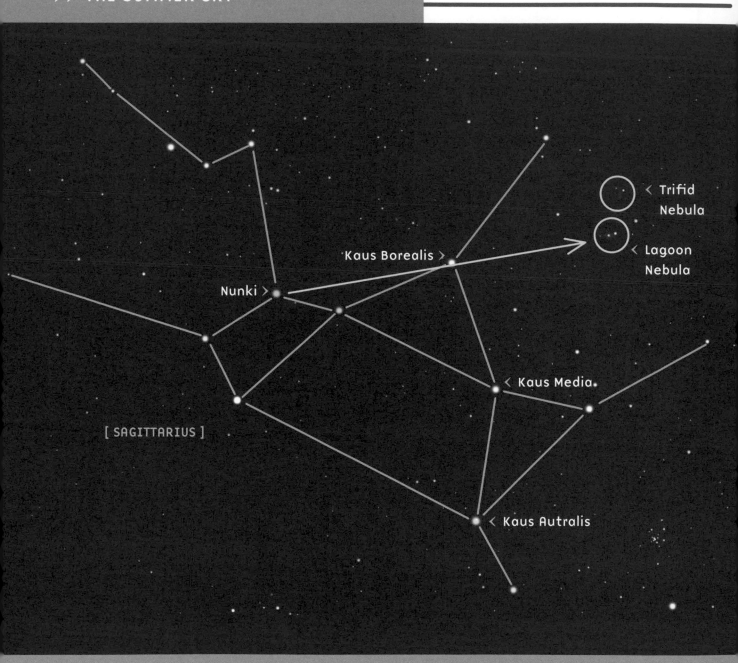

Trifid Nebula

Lagoon Nebula

Kaus Borealis

Nunki

Kaus Media

[SAGITTARIUS]

Kaus Autralis

THE LAGOON (M8) AND TRIFID NEBULAE (M20)

The Lagoon and Trifid Nebulae are two different shaped fuzzy patches seen through a telescope. Try to find the Lagoon Nebula first since it can be visible even with only binoculars. Then for more of a challenge, move on to the Trifid. Particularly for the Trifid, you'll want a dark night with a very clear sky. There are also star clusters in the region you may happen to see.

To find the Lagoon Nebula, start with the Teapot asterism of Sagittarius (page 49). Follow a line from the star Nunki at the top of the handle to the star Kaus Borealis at the top of the lid. Now extend that line the same distance to the Lagoon Nebula. The Trifid Nebula will be a much shorter additional distance in the direction shown in the illustration to the left.

> ## THAT'S SO COOL!
> Both the Lagoon Nebula and the Trifid Nebula are star-forming regions where cute baby stars are being born.

> A telescope picture of the Lagoon (lower middle) and Trifid (upper right) nebulae.

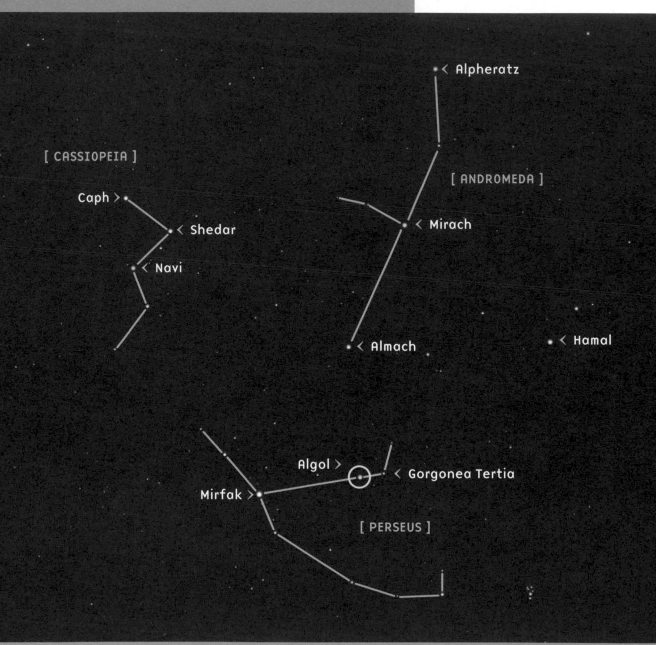

[CASSIOPEIA]

Caph >

< Shedar

< Navi

< Alpheratz

[ANDROMEDA]

< Mirach

< Almach

< Hamal

Algol >   < Gorgonea Tertia

Mirfak >

[PERSEUS]

ALGOL,
A VARIABLE STAR

Algol is the most famous example of a variable star, which is a star whose brightness changes with time. Algol is easy to observe with just your eyes unless you are in a very bright city environment, in which case, try binoculars.

The trick to observing the interesting variability of Algol is to observe it over multiple nights. Algol dims approximately every three days—to be more precise, every two days, 20 hours, and 49 minutes. It dims for a period of about 10 hours, with the maximum dimming about five hours after it starts. Algol is three times brighter at its brightest than it is at its dimmest! Algol dims because it is what is known as an eclipsing binary: two stars that orbit each other and appear to periodically block each other as seen from Earth.

In Algol's case, the dimming occurs when the dimmer star blocks the brighter star.

Algol is in the constellation Perseus, which doesn't have many bright stars. It does have one fairly bright star: Mirfak, which is the brightest star between the constellation Cassiopeia (page 23) and the bright star Capella of the Winter Hexagon (page 25). You can also use some combination of Andromeda (page 53) or the Pleiades (page 33) or Aldebaran (page 31) to find Mirfak and Algol. In the evening, Algol and Perseus will be in the Northeast in the Autumn and overhead in the Winter.

I suggest you observe Algol each night over several nights, perhaps for as much as a week. Compare it with the brightness of other stars to help you see its brightness change. Most of the time it will be about as bright as the star Almach in Andromeda. When it dims, it will be about as bright as the next star beyond Algol

Continued on page 151

> A camera photo of the Perseus region, taken with long exposure to show lots of dim stars. Algol is just left of center, Mirfak at left center, and the Pleiades star cluster appears in the lower right.

Continued from page 149

from Mirfak in Perseus, a star named Gorgonea Tertia. This star is actually somewhat variable over a period of 50 days, but should work for this comparison. To be sure you observe Algol when it is dim—in other words, near a minimum in brightness—check out websites that will calculate those times for your time zone. Search for "Algol minima."

> THAT'S SO COOL!

Because of its changing brightness, many cultures came up with scary names for the star. *Algol* is from the Arabic word for "ghoul." It is often known as the Demon Star. In Hebrew folklore, it was known as Satan's Head.

GLOSSARY

ASTERISM: A pattern of stars in the sky forming a recognizable shape.

ATMOSPHERE: The gases (for example, oxygen and nitrogen) held by gravity to a planet, moon, or other body.

COMET: Icy dirtballs (or dirty iceballs) in space that can be the size of a city; when they come near the Sun, dust and gas come off the surface and form fuzzy-looking objects with tails that can sometimes be seen with eyes, binoculars, or telescopes.

CONSTELLATION: One of 88 internationally agreed-upon patterns of stars; each constellation is given boundaries, dividing the total sky into 88 areas.

DOUBLE STAR: Two stars that appear close to each other through a telescope, often appearing as a single star to just your eyes.

GALAXY: A collection of millions, billions, or even trillions of stars, as well as dust and gas, all held together in one group by gravity. We live in the Milky Way Galaxy.

GLOBULAR CLUSTER: A spherical (ball-shaped) dense collection of hundreds of thousands of stars, usually older stars. The stars not only appear near one another in the sky but also are actually near one another in space.

LIGHT YEAR: A measure of distance, not time. It is the distance light travels in space in one year, equal to about 5.9 trillion miles (5,900,000,000,000 miles) or 9.5 trillion kilometers (9,500,000,000,000 kilometers). This measurement is used in astronomy because stars and galaxies are really far away.

LUNAR ECLIPSE: An event when the Moon is exactly on the opposite side of Earth from the Sun, causing the Moon to enter Earth's shadow.

MAGNIFICATION: A number that represents how much bigger an object appears when looking through binoculars or a telescope.

METEOR: A streak of light in the sky caused by space stuff burning up as it hits the upper atmosphere of the Earth at very high speeds. Note: a meteorite is what we call a rock that makes it through the atmosphere to the surface of Earth.

MOON: An object that orbits a planetary body; moons are often called natural satellites. The Earth's moon is known as the Moon.

NEBULA: A giant collection of dust and gas in space; some nebulae are left over from material blown outward during the end stages of stars, while others are star-forming regions.

OPEN CLUSTER: A group of up to a few thousand stars that are rather spread out in the sky (compared with a globular cluster) that formed from the same giant cloud of gas and dust at a similar time in the past. The stars not only appear near one another in the sky but also are actually near one another in space.

ORBIT: The path a planet or moon or other object follows as it goes around another object; for example, the Earth's orbit around the Sun is approximately a circle.

PLANET: Originally, one of the five "wandering" star-like objects in the night sky (Mercury, Venus, Mars, Jupiter, and Saturn) that move relative to the stars.

Since the telescope was invented, the definition has varied. Now it is an object that orbits the Sun that is rounded by gravity and has "cleared the neighborhood" of its orbit of any objects of similar size.

PLANETARY NEBULA: A shell of ionized (electrically charged) gas that was blasted off a star during the last stages of its life when it was a so-called red giant. Planetary nebulae have nothing to do with planets, but were named that because very early telescopic astronomers thought some looked like planets.

RED GIANT: One of the end phases of the life of a middle- to low-mass star in which the star expands (becomes giant) and as a result, its surface cools, causing the red color.

STAR: An enormous ball of hot glowing gas (technically plasma, which is electrically charged gas). The Sun is a star. All stars except the Sun are so far away that they appear as dots of light in the night sky.

STAR CLUSTER: A group of stars that not only appear near one another in the sky but are also actually near one another in space.

SOLAR ECLIPSE: An event that occurs when the Moon is exactly between the Sun and the Earth, causing the Moon's shadow to cross part of the Earth.

SUPERNOVA: The explosion of a huge star at the end of its normal life, causing brightening over weeks and months and years.

SUPERNOVA REMNANT: The gas and dust left over from the supernova explosion of a huge star at the end of its life.

VARIABLE STAR: A star whose brightness changes with time over days, weeks, months, or years.

RESOURCES

WHERE TO LOOK FOR PLANETS, SKY CHARTS, AND MORE

Sky and Telescope magazine's website: Skyandtelescope.com. In particular, check out "This Week's Sky at a Glance." Look on the menu under Interactive Tools to find a sky chart creator, Jupiter moon position information, and other useful tools. You can also find telescope buying guide information. You can also subscribe to their magazine, which includes upcoming sky information and star charts.

Astronomy magazine's website: Astronomy.com. In particular, check out "Sky This Week." You can also subscribe to their magazine, which includes upcoming sky information and star charts.

Planetary Radio: Planetary.org/radio. Listen to this weekly podcast/radio show for night sky info, as well as space facts and a trivia contest. You can listen to the author of this book in the last few minutes of each show.

Stellarium (free night sky software for PC, Mac, or Linux): Stellarium.org. Make sure you set your city as your default location when you use it. Many other paid software programs also exist and can be purchased from Amazon or astronomy websites.

Night sky apps for iOS and Android can be found by searching the appropriate app store. An app based on Stellarium is available for a small purchase price.

You can buy a planisphere, which is a handheld adjustable sky chart, on Amazon, from a telescope or astronomy website, or some stores. Make sure it generally matches your latitude (or is for mid-Northern latitudes, assuming that is where you live).

INFORMATION ABOUT THE NEXT ECLIPSES

NASA's eclipse webpages: Eclipse.gsfc.nasa.gov/eclipse.html

The Planetary Society: Your guide to future total solar eclipses. Here's an article about all total solar eclipses until 2030: Planetary.org/eclipse

METEOR SHOWER INFORMATION

American Meteor Society Meteor Shower Calendar: AMSMeteors.org /meteor-showers/meteor-shower-calendar

Astronomy Calendar of Events for the current year (includes all types of celestial events): Seasky.org/astronomy/astronomy-calendar-current.html

INTERNATIONAL SPACE STATION FLYOVERS

NASA's Spot the Station (make sure you enter your city!): SpotTheStation.nasa.gov

Heavens Above (make sure you enter your city!): Heavens-Above.com. The site also has predictions for other satellites, sky charts, and other information.

FIND YOUR LOCAL ASTRONOMY CLUB OR ORGANIZATION

NASA/JPL Night Sky Network list of clubs and events: NightSky.jpl.nasa.gov/club-map.cfm

Sky and Telescope: SkyAndTelescope.com/astronomy-clubs-organizations

The Astronomical League: https://www.astroleague.org/astronomy-clubs-usa-state

TELESCOPE BRANDS

Celestron, Meade, and Orion are examples of commonly used telescope brands. Each brand has different specifications and will be better for different viewing purposes. Review your sky-viewing needs to help find the best telescope for your night sky watching.

GENERAL SPACE EXPLORATION INFORMATION AND FUN

The Planetary Society: Planetary.org. Visit this website to get space exploration updates and to join the world's largest space interest group.

Random Space Fact: RandomSpaceFact.com. Dr. Bruce Betts's website offers information about the author and links to his other astronomy-related content, including videos, a radio show, classes, and social media accounts.

The Planetary Society's *Random Space Fact with Dr. Bruce Betts*: Planetary.org/rsf. This website offers fun, humorous, short videos full of space facts.

The Planetary Society's Introduction to Planetary Science and Astronomy Course: Planetary.org/bettsclass. Take Dr. Bruce Betts's introductory college astronomy course for free online.

NASA Space Place: SpacePlace.nasa.gov. This website, designed for kids, lets visitors learn about space and enjoy space-related activities.

NASA Kids Club: NASA.gov/kidsclub/index.html. Visit this page for games and information about NASA.

ASTRONOMY AND NIGHT SKY BOOKS

Consolmagno, Guy and Dan M. Davis. *Turn Left at Orion: Hundreds of Night Sky Objects to See in a Home Telescope—and How to Find Them*. New York: Cambridge University Press, 2011.

Read, John A. *50 Things to See with a Telescope Kids and Parents, Too*. 2017.

Regas, Dean. *100 Things to See in the Night Sky: From Planets and Satellites to Meteors and Constellations, Your Guide to Stargazing*. New York: Adams Media, 2017.

Seronik, Gary. *Binocular Highlights: 99 Celestial Sights for Binocular Users*. Cambridge, MA: Sky & Telescope Media, 2012.

INDEX OF OBJECTS

INDEX

ACKNOWLEDGMENTS

Thanks to Jennifer Vaughn for her wise professional guidance and her magnificent love and support. Thanks to my sons, Kevin and Daniel Betts, for their support of projects like this as well as for bringing happiness and fulfillment to my life. I am grateful to my parents, Bert A. and Barbara Lang Betts, for supporting my early interest in space and education, and to Kathleen Reagan Betts for her excellent Mom-ness to our sons. And thank you to Bill Nye and all the staff and supporters of the Planetary Society for their interest in and support of my broader science and education efforts.

Thanks to my editor, Susan Randol, for all of her suggestions and comments that have made this a better book, and for being a pleasure to work with. My appreciation goes out to Merideth Harte, Amy Hartmann, Vanessa Putt, Andrew Yackira, Oriana Siska, and the rest of the Callisto Media team for their positive attitudes and professional efforts that enabled this book and made it better. And thanks to Erica L. Colón for the wonderful foreword. Finally, thanks to all the readers of this book for giving it a try and for embracing the joy of Astronomy. Enjoy!

ABOUT THE AUTHOR

DR. BRUCE BETTS is a planetary scientist who loves teaching people about planets, space, and the night sky in fun and entertaining ways. He has lots of college degrees, lots of big dogs, and two sons.

Dr. Betts is the chief scientist and LightSail program manager for the world's largest space interest group, the Planetary Society. He has a bachelor's degree in physics and math and a master's degree in applied physics with an emphasis in astronomy from Stanford University. He earned his PhD in planetary science with a minor in geology from the California Institute of Technology. His research there and at the Planetary Science Institute focused on infrared studies of planetary surfaces. He also managed planetary instrument development programs at NASA headquarters.

At the Planetary Society, he heads both the Science and Technology and the Education and Outreach programs. He has managed several flight hardware projects and led additional science and outreach projects. He regularly writes for the member magazine the *Planetary Report* and his blog on Planetary.org. His popular Twitter feed (@RandomSpaceFact) and Facebook page (Facebook .com/DrBruceBetts) provide night sky astronomy and random space facts. His *Random Space Fact* video series (Planetary.org/rsf) provides space facts mixed with humor and graphics. He also hosts the "What's Up?" feature on the weekly Planetary Radio show (Planetary.org/radio) (100+ stations, XM/Sirius, podcast). He has been a guest expert on History Channel's *The Universe*, is a frequent contributor to *Professional Pilot* magazine, and has appeared frequently in TV, print, web media, and public lectures. Dr. Betts is an adjunct professor with California

State University, Dominguez Hills. His Introduction to Astronomy and Planetary Science class, featuring lots of awe-inspiring space pictures, is available for free online (Planetary.org/bettsclass). He is an alumnus senior scientist with the Planetary Science Institute. Visit his website at RandomSpaceFact.com.

The author used Stellarium (stellarium.org), a free and open-source stargazing program, to create the star maps shown throughout this book. The full sky milky way panorama has been created by Axel Mellinger, University of Potsdam, Germany. Further information and more pictures available from MilkyWaySky.com